Mindset

Learning and Living the Will of God

An Inductive Study of Romans 8

by

pam gillaspie

Dedicated to the memory of . . .

Bonnie Ness, a true lover of God, a good and faithful servant of God and man.

**Mindset: Learning and Living the Will
of God**

Copyright © 2025 Pam Gillaspie
Published by Ignite Bible Ministries
www.pamgillaspie.com

ISBN978-1-960938-07-7

Printed in the United States of America

2025

Mindset

Learning and Living the Will of God

Let me sum up *Sweeter than Chocolate!*® Bible studies for you in two words—flexible and joyful!

This Bible study series is designed to flex with your life and give you the option to go as deep as you desire each week. If you're just starting out and feeling a little overwhelmed, stick with the main text and don't think twice about the sidebar assignments. But if you're looking for a challenge, take the sidebar prompts, roll up your sleeves, and dig to your heart's content! As you move along through the study, think of the sidebars and *Digging Deeper* boxes as the elastic that will help this study fit you perfectly.

Did you know that a little flexibility can bring a lot of joy? When a study has the ability to flex to meet you, an amazing thing happens. Guilt starts to melt away and pursuing God through His Word takes on a new sense of joy. What was once a hard obligation becomes a sweet opportunity to commune with God.

So whether you're new to the Book or have been studying it for years, this joy-based study will flex to meet you where you are and push you as far as you care to go . . . and maybe even one step further!

Life has a way of ebbing and flowing and this study is designed to ebb and flow right along with it!

Enjoy!

Mindset
Learning and Living the Will of God

An Inductive Study of Romans 8

How to use this study

Sweeter than Chocolate!® studies meet you where you are and take you as far as you want to go.

1. WEEKLY STUDY: The main text guides you through the complete topic of study for the week.

2. FYI boxes: For Your Information boxes provide bite-sized material to shed additional light on the topic.

> **FYI:**
>
> **Reading Tip: Begin with Prayer**
>
> You may have heard this a million times over and if this is a million and one, so be it. Whenever you read or study God's Word, first pray and ask His Spirit to be your Guide.

3. ONE STEP FURTHER and other sidebar boxes: Sidebar boxes give you the option to push yourself a little further. If you have extra time or are looking for an extra challenge, you can try one, all, or any number in between! These boxes give you the ultimate in flexibility.

> **ONE STEP FURTHER:**
>
> **Word Study: *torah* / law**
>
> The first of eight Hebrew key words we encounter for God's Word is *torah* translated "law." If you're up for a challenge this week, do a word study to learn what you can about *torah*. Run a concordance search and examine where the word *torah* appears in the Old Testament and see what you can learn about from the contexts.
>
> If you decide to look for the word for "law" in the New Testament, you'll find that the primary Greek word is *nomos*.
>
> Be sure to see what Paul says about the law in Galatians 3 and what Jesus says in Matthew 5.

4. DIGGING DEEPER boxes: If you're looking to go further, Digging Deeper sections will help you sharpen your skills as you continue to mine the truths of Scripture for yourself.

> ## Digging Deeper
>
> **What else does God's Word say about counselors?**
>
> If you can, spend some time this week digging around for what God's Word says about counselors.
>
> Start by considering what you already know about counsel from the Word of God and see if you can show where these truths are in the Bible. Make sure that the Word actually says what you think it says.

Living on Purpose

. . . in all these things we overwhelmingly conquer
through Him who loved us.
—Romans 8:37

It is the best seller every year as far back as they've been keeping score. No piece of literature, ancient or modern, rivals the Bible—God's very words recorded for men and women to learn not only about Him, but also about themselves and how to practically live, not only well, but above the pack as more than conquerors! But questions abound—*How do I start? How does it all fit together? How do I go about understanding such a big Book? And while we're at it, how can I find all those life answers people tell me are in there?*

Romans 8, which sits smack dab in the middle of the book of Romans, gives us a one-chapter look at the heart of biblical theology. Don't choke on those words! Biblical theology is simply a way of describing how we understand the main teachings in the Bible—teachings that inform us how to survive and thrive on the planet while eagerly awaiting the mind-blowing future God has in store for us! Understanding creation (how God made the world), sin and the broken condition we find ourselves in, salvation and how God is bringing it about, and then glimpsing into the future He has prepared all work together to help us live purposefully and victoriously today.

The ironic thing about theology is that while the categories and phrases often used to talk about it—soteriology, eschatology, -ology, -ology, -ology—cause a spontaneous eye glaze in many people, the issues theology addresses can wake the dead. *How did we get here? Is there a purpose to life? Am I broken beyond repair or is there hope for me? Are good and evil equal duelling powers? Is anyone in control? How can I live as more than a conqueror?* and those, my friend are just the start.

So what are we waiting for? Let's get started!

FYI:

If You're in a Class

Complete **Lesson One** together on your first day of class. This will be a great way to start getting to know one another and will help those who are newer to Bible study get their bearings.

Learning and Living the Will of God

An Inductive Study of Romans 8

CONSIDER the WAY you THINK

What life questions do you hope the Bible answers?

FYI:

There's No Question Too Big for God

I have a degree in biblical studies and I learned much in college that laid a solid foundation for what has become a life-time of studying the Bible. Probably the most significant truth came in the first semester of my freshmen year in a theology class required of all students. The professor told us there is no question too big for God. We don't have to fear asking the one question that will somehow "undo" Him. He is the sovereign God! He is big enough to stand up to all of our doubts, to all of our questions.

That doesn't mean we'll find answers to absolutely every question. The secret things belong to God; He's revealed all we need to know (Deuteronomy 29:29). There will always be some mystery because we are limited in our ability to understand. But we can press into Him with confidence that He is big enough to stand up to whatever questions we have.

Nothing catches Him by surprise. Nothing catches Him at a loss of power. Nothing catches Him with an inability to respond. This doesn't mean life always turns up rainbows and butterflies. The Book tells us it won't. Yet even in the midst of terrible and painful situations, we can choose to remember—as hard as it may be at times—the truths of both the sovereignty and goodness of God.

Have you ever seriously looked at the Bible in order to answer these questions? Why/why not?

Where do you typically look for answers to life's big questions? How satisfied have you been with the answers you've found?

What is your view of the Bible? Do you believe it is God's Word or are you still wrestling (or maybe just starting to wrestle!) with this issue?

Digging Deeper

Examining the Context for Yourself

In the next section, I'm going to give you basic background information on the book of Romans. Before I tip my hand, though, if you have time it would be great for you to read it and consider general questions on your own.

If you choose to dig information out for yourself, you'll want to pay attention and look for answers to specific questions. I've given you some direction below. In the parenthesis you'll find terms commentators attach to these basic questions we want to address to any book in the Bible we're studying.

Who wrote the book of Romans? Is this clear or questionable? Explain. (Author)

Who was it written to? Where were these people located? Was it a homogenous or mixed group of people? (Recipient/Destination)

When was it written? What facts lead you to this date or date range? (Date)

What historical context clues does the text give about the culture at the time of writing?

Why was Romans written? (Occasion/Purpose)

Where was the author when he wrote it? Why do you think this? What facts support your answer? (Place of Origin)

What are some key words that you've noticed? What are some significant themes?

Overviewing the Text

Pastor John Piper talks about how we should "pray and ransack" the Bible as we look for truth. I love this counsel. We don't just casually read over the words; we fully engage and seek to plumb the riches of the Word and find every last morsel God has for us. As we overview the text, we begin the respectful ransacking process of asking questions, turning over rocks, and looking for treasures in the Word.

You can check out the full article at this address: http://www.desiringgod. org/ResourceLibrary/Sermons/By-Date/1998/1025_Wonderful_Things_ From_Your_Word/

BACKGROUND INFORMATION on ROMANS

While our focus in this study is Romans 8, we need to examine the context and gain an understanding of the basics of the letter to the Romans. What are the basics? We're looking in the text for who wrote the letter and to whom. We want to know as closely as possible when and where the letter was written. We also want to know what the occasion was—why the author penned the letter. To help set these context questions in your head, we'll look at them individually below. They're not always easy to answer and sometimes we have to settle for "God knows, but I don't." Who authored the book of Hebrews, for instance, remains a mystery. For Romans, however, internal evidences are reasonably clear.

Authorship

Nearly all scholars liberal and conservative agree that Paul wrote the book of Romans. The book bears his name and even critical scholars accept Romans as Paul's work. The closing chapter indicates that Tertius scribed the letter (Romans 16:22), but the content is certainly Pauline.

Recipients

Paul wrote to the "beloved of God in Rome," obviously a reference to the church. A difficult follow-up question is, "What was the makeup of the church?" The letter itself suggests the church was comprised of both Jewish and Gentile believers in Jesus Christ.

Occasion

On a very basic level Paul writes that he is planning to visit Rome (Romans 1:10-11). Romans is not a follow-up letter to a church Paul has either established or visited. Rather, it is a greeting sent prior to his coming.

Place of Origin

Paul probably wrote to the Romans from Corinth toward the end of his third missionary journey, but some scholars also suggest Ephesus as the place of origin.

Date

Paul may have written the book of Romans as early as 54 AD, but the strongest evidence suggests a time frame of AD 57 to 59. Acts and extra-biblical records for officials and rulers confirm Paul first visited Rome about AD 60. This implies Romans was written prior to that, probably before his imprisonment in Caesarea, so AD 57 to 59 has solid foundation.

FYI:

Why the Background Matters

Whenever we study Scripture, it's critical to pay attention to context. While we're focusing our attention on Romans 8, we need to keep in mind that it is part of a greater whole. Knowing the background is part of staying attentive to context.

FYI:

"God said it" settles it for me . . .

Since you're doing this study my best guess is that "God said it" settles matters for you, too. So when the text of Scripture says Paul wrote Romans, we're satisfied. Thing is, though, not everyone takes God at His Word. If you encounter someone with doubts about the Bible, Romans is a great place to direct them because even liberal scholars accept its authenticity. Does this mean we call into question every book of the Bible? Absolutely not! I take what God says at face value and trust it, but I also want to know enough about how other people think so I can best engage them where they are and hopefully encourage them on their path toward God.

OBSERVE the TEXT of SCRIPTURE

READ Romans 8. **CIRCLE** every reference to the *Spirit*; **UNDERLINE** every reference to the *flesh*; and **WATCH** for other key words.

Romans 8

1   Therefore there is now no condemnation for those who are in Christ Jesus.

2   For the law of the Spirit of life in Christ Jesus has set you free from the law of sin and of death.

3   For what the Law could not do, weak as it was through the flesh, God did: sending His own Son in the likeness of sinful flesh and as an offering *for sin,* He condemned sin in the flesh,

4   so that the requirement of the Law might be fulfilled in us, who do not walk according to the flesh but according to the Spirit.

5   For those who are according to the flesh set their minds on the things of the flesh, but those who are according to the Spirit, the things of the Spirit.

6   For the mind set on the flesh is death, but the mind set on the Spirit is life and peace,

7   because the mind set on the flesh is hostile toward God; for it does not subject itself to the law of God, for it is not even able to do so,

8   and those who are in the flesh cannot please God.

9   However, you are not in the flesh but in the Spirit, if indeed the Spirit of God dwells in you. But if anyone does not have the Spirit of Christ, he does not belong to Him.

10 If Christ is in you, though the body is dead because of sin, yet the spirit is alive because of righteousness.

11 But if the Spirit of Him who raised Jesus from the dead dwells in you, He who raised Christ Jesus from the dead will also give life to your mortal bodies through His Spirit who dwells in you.

12 So then, brethren, we are under obligation, not to the flesh, to live according to the flesh—

13 for if you are living according to the flesh, you must die; but if by the Spirit you are putting to death the deeds of the body, you will live.

14 For all who are being led by the Spirit of God, these are sons of God.

15 For you have not received a spirit of slavery leading to fear again, but you have received a spirit of adoption as sons by which we cry out, "Abba! Father!"

16 The Spirit Himself testifies with our spirit that we are children of God,

---

FYI:

Keeping First Things First

Whenever you come to God's Word to study or read, don't forget to pray before you begin. Why? Because Jesus said, "But when He, the Spirit of truth, comes, He will guide you into all the truth; for He will not speak on His own initiative, but whatever He hears, He will speak; and He will disclose to you what is to come. He will glorify Me, for He will take of Mine and will disclose *it* to you" (John 16:13-14). When you sit down to dive in, ask the Spirit to guide you. Jesus said He would, so take Him at His word and ask.

INDUCTIVE FOCUS:

What is a Key Word?

A key word unlocks the meaning of a text. Key words are sometimes repeated and are critical to the message of the passage. As you read through Romans 8, several repeated key words will probably pop out at you. Watch for words that cluster within a few verses and are key to sections of the text. If you don't see them right away, don't worry. I'll help by pointing some out as we go. Identifying key words is a skill that develops over time, but you practice by observing carefully. So keep your eyes opened. You will get it, just keep praying and keep looking.

Mindset
Learning and Living the Will of God

An Inductive Study of Romans 8

INDUCTIVE FOCUS:

Key Words: Spirit and Flesh

You'll quickly notice *spirit* and *flesh* appearing throughout Romans 8. Other important words appear clustered in sections. As you identify clusters, it will help you remember the flow of the text. Here are a few to keep an eye on and consider marking. Some of the reference ranges below *do* overlap—it's intentional!

1-4	law, condemn/condemnation
5-8	mind set/set their minds
9-13	dwells, alive/live/life, die
14-23	adoption, children, sons, heirs
16-25	creation, hope, glory/glorified, waits eagerly, suffer/sufferings, groans
26-34	intercedes
34-39	separate, love, negative conjunctions

17 and if children, heirs also, heirs of God and fellow heirs with Christ, if indeed we suffer with Him so that we may also be glorified with Him.

18 For I consider that the sufferings of this present time are not worthy to be compared with the glory that is to be revealed to us.

19 For the anxious longing of the creation waits eagerly for the revealing of the sons of God.

20 For the creation was subjected to futility, not willingly, but because of Him who subjected it,
in hope

21 that the creation itself also will be set free from its slavery to corruption into the freedom of the glory of the children of God.

22 For we know that the whole creation groans and suffers the pains of childbirth together until now.

23 And not only this, but also we ourselves, having the first fruits of the Spirit, even we ourselves groan within ourselves, waiting eagerly for our adoption as sons, the redemption of our body.

24 For in hope we have been saved, but hope that is seen is not hope; for who hopes for what he already sees?

25 But if we hope for what we do not see, with perseverance we wait eagerly for it.

26 In the same way the Spirit also helps our weakness; for we do not know how to pray as we should, but the Spirit Himself intercedes for us with groanings too deep for words;

27 and He who searches the hearts knows what the mind of the Spirit is, because He intercedes for the saints according to the will of God.

28 And we know that God causes all things to work together for good to those who love God, to those who are called according to His purpose.

29 For those whom He foreknew, He also predestined to become conformed to the image of His Son, so that He would be the firstborn among many brethren;

30 and these whom He predestined, He also called; and these whom He called, He also justified; and these whom He justified, He also glorified.

31 What then shall we say to these things? If God is for us, who is against us?

32 He who did not spare His own Son, but delivered Him over for us all, how will He not also with Him freely give us all things?

33 Who will bring a charge against God's elect? God is the one who justifies;

34 who is the one who condemns? Christ Jesus is He who died, yes, rather who was raised, who is at the right hand of God, who also intercedes for us.

35 Who will separate us from the love of Christ? Will tribulation, or distress, or persecution, or famine, or nakedness, or peril, or sword?

36 Just as it is written,

"FOR YOUR SAKE WE ARE BEING PUT TO DEATH ALL DAY LONG;

WE WERE CONSIDERED AS SHEEP TO BE SLAUGHTERED."

37 But in all these things we overwhelmingly conquer through Him who loved us.

38 For I am convinced that neither death, nor life, nor angels, nor principalities, nor things present, nor things to come, nor powers,

39 nor height, nor depth, nor any other created thing, will be able to separate us from the love of God, which is in Christ Jesus our Lord.

DISCUSS with your GROUP or PONDER on your own . . .

What are your initial observations on the text?

What important word opens up Romans 8? What does it refer back to?

What is the earliest biblical event alluded to in Romans 8?

What other broad time periods does Paul refer to? (This is a general question, don't overanalyze—think broadly!)

Marking the Text

Marking the text is a tool that can help you draw the meaning out of the text, particularly if you are a visual learner. If you're uncomfortable marking the text of your Bible, practicing on the text in your workbook is a great way to try the tool.

There is nothing magical about the process. Doing it doesn't make you a better student, just as not doing it doesn't make you a worse student. There are excellent Bible scholars who don't use colored pencils to mark the text just like there are others who use colored pencils and don't handle the Word well.

Marking shows repetition and an author's emphasis—what's important in his message—and leads to understanding subjects and flow of thought.

What is the *therefore* there for?

Whenever we find a *therefore* in text, we need to ask this question: "What is the *therefore* there for?" Because a *therefore* shows up in Romans 8:1, we need to look in the chapter(s) preceding it to answer this important question.

Mindset
Learning and Living the Will of God
An Inductive Study of Romans 8

Lesson One: **Living on Purpose**

Look back through the whole chapter and list the benefits that come to people who walk according to the Spirit. In another column, list the condition of those who walk according to the flesh. It will be helpful for your discussion time if you record the verse numbers where you find your answers.

SPIRIT	FLESH

INDUCTIVE TIP:

Think Color Schemes

As you start becoming comfortable with **marking** key words, consider other **markings** to help you identify things such as patterns or groups within the text.

In Romans 8, for instance, there's a huge contrast between two ways of living and the resultant outcomes. *Spirit, life, peace,* and *righteousness* sit on one side of the aisle while *flesh, death, hostility,* and *law* are juxtaposed on the other. If you're using colored pencils, you may want to highlight the *spirit/life* words and results with one color and the *law/death* words and results in another.

This is just another way you can **mark** the text. You can still **mark** individual key words and then hit related word groups with a common color.

Again, if you hate **marking** either forget I mentioned this or, better yet, try this as a simple first step in **marking** the text. You may be pleasantly surprised by the results! **Marking** doesn't make the text say something different, but it can help make what it *does say* stand out more clearly.

By the way, any idea what the key word in this sidebar is?

How appealing is life in the Spirit? What specifics appeal to you the most?

From what you have observed in the church, do the lives of most professing Christians resemble the "life in the Spirit" described in Romans 8? Explain. How can this affect those outside of the faith?

Why don't you take a few minutes right now and ask God to guide you through this class and help you to rest in the work He is doing in you as He conforms you to the image of Christ, continually aligning your heart more and more with His.

TRUE STORIES:

Acts: The Arrival of the Spirit

While we see the presence of the Holy Spirit throughout the pages of the Bible, there is a fundamental shift in the book of Acts. Before the day of Pentecost, the Spirit was given to certain people for certain tasks, but never to God's people as a whole. At Pentecost, everything changes. Jesus told his disciples in John 16:5-15 that when He goes away, He will send the Spirit to guide them into all truth. His Words are fulfilled in Acts 2. If you have some extra time, read John 16:5-15 to hear Jesus' words about the Spirit first hand. If you're really up for some reading, work your way through the book of Acts and observe how the presence of the Holy Spirit changes the timid disciples. Record your observations below.

FLASH BACK, FLASH FORWARD, FLASH SIDEWAYS . . .

Now that we've established an overall look at Romans 8, it's time to buckle in. As we've seen, Paul flashes back to creation, flashes forward to the glory to come and also talks about this present life. He's candid about not only the extreme benefit of being in Christ but also of the present suffering that goes with it as well.

In order to understand how the past and the future impact how we live today, we're going to examine the biblical time periods and concepts he refers to for ourselves. We'll flash back with him to the creation story in Genesis, we'll flash forward with him to the future hope and we'll look at how all of it affects the here and now—how we can live lives of God-focused purpose and influence in a fallen world.

As we move on this week, let's take our first flashback. Romans 8 talks quite a bit about creation, which presupposes a Creator. While we'll flash back even further a little later in the study when we consider God's foreknowledge, for today we'll start in Genesis.

OBSERVE the TEXT of SCRIPTURE

READ Genesis 1–2 in your Bible paying close attention to repeated words and phrases that describe God's activity in and His estimation of creation. Record your observations below, then I'll ask a few questions. As always, I'm hoping you'll be asking questions of the text independently (*before* you find them in this study guide).

DISCUSS with your GROUP or PONDER on your own . . .

What does the Genesis account assume about the beginning of the world?

ONE STEP FURTHER:

Word Study: Creation

If you have some time this week, look closely at the usage of the word *creation* in Romans 8 and compare that with its usage in the rest of Romans, the other writings of Paul, and the rest of the Bible. After you have done your own study, consult word study resources including bible dictionaries and commentaries. Record your findings below.

Does Genesis try in any way to explain creation beyond attributing it to God?

What do we do with this in a world that assumes evolution? What options do we have as we engage our culture and teach the next generation?

Start with Prayer

You've probably heard it before and if we study together in the future, you're sure to hear it again. Whenever you read or study God's Word, first pray and ask His Spirit to be your Guide. It's one way to purposefully set your mind on the things of the Spirit.

What phrase does God repeatedly use to describe what He created? How does He describe His creation of man?

What is significantly different in man as opposed to the rest of creation? What characteristic sets man apart from the rest of creation?

Does this fit the evolutionary worldview? Why or why not?

Lesson One: **Living on Purpose**

OBSERVE the TEXT of SCRIPTURE

READ Romans 1:20 and **UNDERLINE** what Paul says people know about God simply from looking at creation. We'll look at the greater context of Romans 1 next week, but for now let's focus on what this verse says about creation.

Romans 1:20

20 *For since the creation of the world His invisible attributes, His eternal power and divine nature, have been clearly seen, being understood through what has been made, so that they are without excuse.*

FYI:

What's up with the open-ended questions?

If you haven't noticed yet, I often pose an open-ended question after you observe a passage of Scripture. Why is that? I want to give you the opportunity to get your thoughts down before tipping my hand to what I've seen in the text. This will help you reason through the text more and more for yourself.

DISCUSS with your GROUP or PONDER on your own . . .

According to Romans 1:20, what can people know about God simply by looking at creation?

How does belief or disbelief in a Creator frame a person's entire worldview?

If the world came about through a set of random occurrences, is there any room for concrete hope in the future? Explain your answer.

Digging Deeper

What does it mean to "set the mind"?

In the text of Romans 8:5-7, we see a form of the phrase "set the mind" or "the mind that is set" appearing four times over the span of just three verses. The mind set one way is death, while the mind set the other way is life. If you have some extra time this week, examine the Greek phrases involved more closely to see where else they are used in Romans and in the rest of the Word of God.

What Greek words are used in these key phrases in Romans 8?

Where do they occur and how are they used?

Where else do these word appear together in Paul's writings?

Do they appear in the Gospels? If so, where and under what circumstances?

INDUCTIVE FOCUS:

Questioning the Text

The key to exegesis (the fancy word meaning to draw meaning out of Scripture) is questioning the text. The basic investigative questions *Who? What? When? Where? Why?* and *How?* are your framework. Not every question can be addressed to every verse, and most verses require several variations on the same question. As we study God's Word together, realize that not every question that can be asked will be asked, but don't let that stop you from asking other questions and exploring further on your own. We will never run out of questions to ask and answers to glean from God's Word!

If you're at a loss for what questions to ask, pay attention to the words that you've marked. Go to your key words and start there with your questions! Marking not only helps you see the main idea, it always helps in asking questions.

Mindset
Learning and Living the Will of God

An Inductive Study of Romans 8

Does this word group show up elsewhere in the New Testament?

Do we see this concept in the Old Testament?

From your study, what does setting one's mind on the Spirit mean?

What, if any, additional insights have you gained from word study books and commentaries?

@THE END OF THE DAY . . .

Romans 8 can be simultaneously encouraging and convicting. We still live in a fallen world where on some days following God is incredibly hard work. But God through His Spirit gives us everything we need to live and live abundantly with our minds set on His ways. Through His Word and His Spirit we can learn more and more to view the world biblically and live purposefully even in the face of suffering when hope seems far off.

As you close out your study this week, take some quiet time (perhaps 30 minutes to an hour) and talk to God about what you've learned so far in Romans 8. Ask Him to cement specific truths to your heart as He begins to change the way you look at life to conform it more and more to the way of His heart. Record any additional thoughts below.

"Indeed, has God said?"

Now the serpent was more crafty than any beast
of the field which the LORD God had made.
And he said to the woman, "Indeed, has God said . . ."
—Genesis 3:1a

We sit in the middle of a clearly damaged world. Just a passing glance at the evening news confirms the reach of the damage—from earthquakes and natural disasters to inhabitants who maim and kill. Our world teems with sorrow and tears, death and injustice. If you haven't experienced it yet, unfortunately you will. It's only a matter of time.

In this Lesson we're going to examine how we landed here in the first place and how this affects
everything after it. It all started with a question that caused Eve to reject what God had revealed to her. This was an attack on the revelation and nature of God. Satan's question ("Indeed, has God said?") and lie ("You will not die!") permeate our society today.

Remember, what God created was good but in a moment in a garden everything changed. Sin and death entered when mankind lusted after the knowledge of good and evil. As Paul says in Romans, man "exchanged the truth of God for a lie" (Romans 1:25).

Looking at how sin entered the world and changed the condition of man may sound like a snore. I know. But how we think about this based on a knowledge of the truth or the seduction of a lie will *profoundly* impact how we live. If you're looking for practical truth that matters, it starts here.

FYI:

What You Think Determines How You Live

If you think what you think doesn't matter, think again! Jesus tells us that what is on the inside comes out in our behavior: "the mouth speaks out of that which fills the heart" (Matthew 12:34).

We're not talking "the power of positive thinking" stuff here. We're talking the transformation of minds, the alignment of our minds with God's.

FYI:

Genesis 1:27 and Mankind

Genesis 1:27 tells us:

God created man in His own image,
in the image of God He created him;
male and female He created them.

The reference to "man" in line one is a generic reference to people in general, to mankind. "Male and female" in line three further defines the general word "man." Since God's Word, both in the Old Testament Hebrew and New Testament Greek unapologetically uses the general "man" to refer to all people, we're going to go with that, too. It's biblical and keeps the writing tighter. Really, you can't beat that combination!

Mindset
Learning and Living the Will of God
An Inductive Study of Romans 8

A LITTLE MORE BACKGROUND INFORMATION on ROMANS

The book of Romans provides a well-reasoned approach to the core beliefs of Christianity. In the first three chapters Paul argues that everyone is a sinner—the flat-out heathen, the "religious," and even the Jew. With no exceptions, all sin and fall short of God's glory.

SINNERS summarizes Romans 1–Romans 3:20.

God saves sinners by faith, not by works. Paul points out that God credited righteousness to both Abraham and David apart from works. It is significant that Abraham lived prior to the Law and David lived under it, yet neither was justified by the Law. People don't save themselves; we are saved by God through faith alone.

SAVED summarizes Romans 3:21—Romans 5.

In this next section Paul talks about the Christian life—how we are to live as followers of Christ. In
Romans 6 we see we are no longer slaves to sin but rather slaves to righteousness. Romans 7, for all the theological questions it raises, makes it clear that the Law can never make a person good. Romans 8, our passage, shows us how to live the normal Christian life of walking by the Spirit.

SANCTIFIED summarizes Romans 6–Romans 8.

Romans 9 through Romans 11 discuss the sovereignty of God in salvation and the place of Israel in His salvific work.

SOVEREIGNTY summarizes Romans 9–Romans 11.

Leading off with a big "Therefore," Romans 12 through the end of the letter focuses on God's call to service in light of everything He has done on our behalf. We are not working to earn God's favor, but serving through the power of His indwelling Spirit.

SERVICE summarizes Romans 12–Romans 16.

OBSERVE the TEXT of SCRIPTURE

READ Romans 8:1-4. **CIRCLE** references to *sin* and **UNDERLINE** references to *condemnation*.

Romans 8:1-4

1   *Therefore there is now no condemnation for those who are in Christ Jesus.*

2   *For the law of the Spirit of life in Christ Jesus has set you free from the law of sin and of death.*

3   *For what the Law could not do, weak as it was through the flesh, God did: sending His own Son in the likeness of sinful flesh and as an offering for sin, He condemned sin in the flesh,*

4   *so that the requirement of the Law might be fulfilled in us, who do not walk according to the flesh but according to the Spirit.*

Mindset
Learning and Living the Will of God

An Inductive Study of Romans 8

DISCUSS with your GROUP or PONDER on your own . . .

What are your initial observations on the text?

What questions do you think we need to ask? Are there words you'd like to explore?
Why?

If there is *now no condemnation,* is there anything we can learn from this text about
why condemnation came about in the first place or do we need to look elsewhere?

ONE STEP FURTHER:

Requirement

A man-made requirement is not necessarily just simply by being enacted into
law. God's law, however, is different. The
requirement we see in Romans 8:4 is
not only a requirement but a *righteous*
requirement. If you have some extra
time this week, find the Greek work for
requirement in this verse and explain the
additional shade of meaning the Greek
brings to this particular word. Record
your findings below.

Mindset
Learning and Living the Will of God

An Inductive Study of Romans 8

Where in Romans and elsewhere in the Bible can we look for more information about how we ended up under condemnation?

ONE STEP FURTHER:

Romans 1

If you have some extra time this week, hang out in Romans 1:18-32. Consider what people can clearly see in creation and how they respond to what they clearly see. Also watch for how they view themselves. What do they think they are? What does the text say they are and why? How does natural man respond to truth? Record your findings below.

If you found some cross-references on your own, how did you identify them?

Paul has clearly *explained* sin's origin and judgment in the earlier chapters of Romans, but to *see* the original scene for ourselves we need to go to Genesis 3 where the account of the fall is recorded.

OBSERVE the TEXT of SCRIPTURE

READ all of Genesis 3 in your Bible. Pay close attention to the tactics of the serpent and **UNDERLINE** everything he says in Genesis 3:1-6 which is included below.

Genesis 3:1-6

1 *Now the serpent was more crafty than any beast of the field which the LORD God had made. And he said to the woman, "Indeed, has God said, 'You shall not eat from any tree of the garden'?"*

2 *The woman said to the serpent, "From the fruit of the trees of the garden we may eat;*

3 *but from the fruit of the tree which is in the middle of the garden, God has said, 'You shall not eat from it or touch it, or you will die.' "*

4 *The serpent said to the woman, "You surely will not die!*

5 *"For God knows that in the day you eat from it your eyes will be opened, and you will be like God, knowing good and evil."*

6 *When the woman saw that the tree was good for food, and that it was a delight to the eyes, and that the tree was desirable to make one wise, she took from its fruit and ate; and she gave also to her husband with her, and he ate.*

DISCUSS with your GROUP or PONDER on your own . . .

What did the serpent say to the woman?

What was his tactic? What was he trying to get her to think about God? What was he trying to get her to doubt and then reject?

What did he offer?

ONE STEP FURTHER:

Where can we find wisdom?

The serpent offered a shortcut to wisdom that backfired in epic proportions. What does the Word of God say about how we can go about acquiring wisdom? If you have some time this week, start off with your concordance and see what you can find. Record what you learn below.

Mindset
Learning and Living the Will of God

An Inductive Study of Romans 8

What did Eve observe about the fruit?

What step-by-step path did Eve travel on her way to sinning? What happens from the time she first listens to the serpent to the point at which she gives the fruit to Adam?

Can understanding Eve's path into sin change the way we normally react when faced with temptation to sin?

How did God punish the serpent?

The woman?

The man?

The earth?

Why does it matter? How do these truths change the way you think and act?

Expectations

If our expectations are not grounded in truth, we will find ourselves living lives of continual disappointment. If I expect all drivers to be courteous, I will, more often than not, find myself frustrated on the roadways. If I expect all telemarketers to respect the "Do Not Call" lists, I will growl at the phone several times a day. If I expect the Cubs to win the World Series . . . nevermind. That one is too painful for me to even address.

I trust you see my point. We live in a fallen world. If we accept the truth of this, if we let it inform our thinking, if we expect fallen people to behave like fallen people, our attitudes will be more bent toward compassion than frustration with the minor infractions of life.

Understanding the consequences of the fall should radically affect our expectations of people and our responses to them.

Good, bad, or morally neutral?

So people do wrong things. That's hardly news. But how often do we stop to consider why that is and how the presence of sin affects life and the way we view life? I'll never forget the time my friend Karen and I were writing and teaching a high school Sunday School class on the book of Romans. Each week we'd start off with an ice-breaker question just to get the conversation started. The particular week forever etched on my brain started off innocently enough. We opened the class with what should have been a pretty simple quiz for a group of teenagers raised in the church:

Man is born:
a. Morally good
b. Morally bad
c. Morally neutral

I expected a few responses of "morally neutral," but was shocked when all but one responded "morally good." We had one "morally neutral" but all the rest were "morally good." I'm not sure if I was more shocked or dismayed. I expected to trip up a couple of kids and get a good conversation going, but I had no clue concerning the extent to which these kids had no clue. So when we regathered ourselves, Karen and I spent the next hour unpacking the concept of sin and the condition of man. It may seem like theological trivia, a fact inconsequential to everyday life, but nothing could be farther from the truth.

The Right Place to Find Wisdom

"The fear of the LORD is the beginning of wisdom, And the knowledge of the Holy One is understanding."

—Proverbs 9:10

Mindset
Learning and Living the Will of God
An Inductive Study of Romans 8

If we think people are basically good or even morally neutral our interactions will be influenced by these false premises. One possible outcome, for example, is that we will expect more than they're capable of thinking or doing and our expectations will consistently be dashed. When we don't have truth as our basis of operations, life becomes quickly tangled.

Let's think through some of the basic ramifications of this thinking on how we view the world and operate in it by looking at some examples from the life of Jesus.

OBSERVE the TEXT of SCRIPTURE

READ John 2:23-25. **CIRCLE** every reference to *Jesus* including pronouns and **UNDERLINE** every occurrence of *know*.

John 2:23-25

23 *Now when He was in Jerusalem at the Passover, during the feast, many believed in His name, observing His signs which He was doing.*

24 *But Jesus, on His part, was not entrusting Himself to them, for He knew all men,*

25 *and because He did not need anyone to testify concerning man, for He Himself knew what was in man.*

DISCUSS with your GROUP or PONDER on your own . . .

What did you learn about Jesus?

How were the people responding to Him?

How did His knowledge of men affect His response to them?

There's an interesting play on words in verses 23 and 24: although the people believed (*episteusan* from the root *pisteuo*) in His name, He did not entrust (*episteuen*, also from the root *pisteuo*) Himself to them. How would you describe Jesus' behavior?

Word Study: Shrewd

If you have some extra time this week, look for the Greek word translated *shrewd* in Matthew 10:16 and see what you can find out about what it means to be as shrewd as a serpent. If you need help on how to do a word study, see the **Resources** section at the end of the book. Record your findings below.

Is it surprising to you that Jesus did not entrust Himself to these people? Why/why not? How quick are you to entrust yourself to people? What can you learn from Jesus' example that you can apply in your life?

OBSERVE the TEXT of SCRIPTURE

READ Matthew 10:16-18, words Jesus spoke when He sent His disciples out to do ministry among the people. **UNDERLINE** what He tells them to be and do.

Matthew 10:16-18

16 *"Behold, I send you out as sheep in the midst of wolves; so be shrewd as serpents and innocent as doves.*

17 *"But beware of men, for they will hand you over to the courts and scourge you in their synagogues;*

18 *and you will even be brought before governors and kings for My sake, as a testimony to them and to the Gentiles.*

Mindset
Learning and Living the Will of God
An Inductive Study of Romans 8

DISCUSS with your GROUP or PONDER on your own . . .

How does Jesus describe the situation His disciples will encounter? What dangers does He picture?

How do you think Jesus' world view plays in our politically correct environment today? Is His view of man different from yours?

What does He tell His disciples to be and do?

Digging Deeper

Walk Some More with Jesus

In our main text this week, we've been looking at some specific instances of Jesus drawing boundaries and acting shrewdly as He considers the hearts of men. It's important for us to watch how He deals with people in their fallen condition so we can learn to think and act wisely too. That said, however, we need always to see this held up alongside His profound and sacrificial love. If you have some extra time this week, spend some of it looking at how Jesus interacted with the people He came in contact with. You'll find first-hand accounts in the four Gospels: Matthew, Mark, Luke, and John. Pick one or more and read through it/ them this week observing how Jesus dealt with people.

How would you characterize Jesus' interactions with people overall?

How did He specifically relate to His disciples?

How did He relate to the masses?

How did He interact with the Pharisees?

Describe some of His interactions with Gentiles.

Describe some of His interactions with religious and political leaders.

Did anything surprise you about the way Jesus interacted with people?

What can you begin to apply to your life this week?

Is God really good?

Yes. Not only that, He does good, too, according to Psalm 119:68 and to the witness of the whole of Scripture! From our historical perspective looking back on God's revealed love in Jesus Christ and Adam and Eve's condition before the fall, it is almost incomprehensible that we could doubt the goodness of God. Let's see what the serpent called into question.

OBSERVE the TEXT of SCRIPTURE

READ Genesis 2:2-9 and 15-17 paying special attention to what the garden was like, what trees grew there, and what one command God gave.

Genesis 2:2-9

2   By the seventh day God completed His work which He had done, and He rested on the seventh day from all His work which He had done.

3   Then God blessed the seventh day and sanctified it, because in it He rested from all His work which God had created and made.

4   This is the account of the heavens and the earth when they were created, in the day that the LORD God made earth and heaven.

5   Now no shrub of the field was yet in the earth, and no plant of the field had yet sprouted, for the LORD God had not sent rain upon the earth, and there was no man to cultivate the ground.

6   But a mist used to rise from the earth and water the whole surface of the ground.

7   Then the LORD God formed man of dust from the ground, and breathed into his nostrils the breath of life; and man became a living being.

8   The LORD God planted a garden toward the east, in Eden; and there He placed the man whom He had formed.

9   Out of the ground the LORD God caused to grow every tree that is pleasing to the sight and good for food; the tree of life also in the midst of the garden, and the tree of the knowledge of good and evil.

Genesis 2:15-17

15   Then the LORD God took the man and put him into the garden of Eden to cultivate it and keep it.

16   The LORD God commanded the man, saying, "From any tree of the garden you may eat freely;

17   but from the tree of the knowledge of good and evil you shall not eat, for in the day that you eat from it you will surely die."

Mindset
Learning and Living the Will of God

An Inductive Study of Romans 8

DISCUSS with your GROUP or PONDER on your own . . .

What did the trees in the garden have in common?

What two trees were specifically named? What rule was associated with one of them?

What was the punishment for breaking the rule? Was God clear?

Could they have eaten from the tree of life? (Just askin' . . .)

How did God's truth about the consequence of eating from the tree of the knowledge of good and evil differ from Satan's lie?

What are some of the ways we shun the clear Word of God in favor of a shiny lie? How can we identify the serpent's lies today so we don't fall for the same bait?

There are always consequences . . .

If the sin of Adam and Eve only affected Adam and Eve, we wouldn't be as interested in their story today. But it didn't stop with them. Their sin brought death not only to them but also to their descendants, everyone since. Let's look at Romans 5:12-21 to learn more about this.

OBSERVE the TEXT of SCRIPTURE

READ Romans 5:12-21 and **UNDERLINE** every reference to *death*. **CIRCLE** every reference to *sin*. While this passage is packed with redemption we're going to focus on how we got into the mess we're in and what ramifications this has for us.

Romans 5:12-21

12 *Therefore, just as through one man sin entered into the world, and death through sin, and so death spread to all men, because all sinned—*

13 *for until the Law sin was in the world, but sin is not imputed when there is no law.*

14 *Nevertheless death reigned from Adam until Moses, even over those who had not sinned in the likeness of the offense of Adam, who is a type of Him who was to come.*

15 *But the free gift is not like the transgression. For if by the transgression of the one the many died, much more did the grace of God and the gift by the grace of the one Man, Jesus Christ, abound to the many.*

16 *The gift is not like that which came through the one who sinned; for on the one hand the judgment arose from one transgression resulting in condemnation, but on the other hand the free gift arose from many transgressions resulting in justification.*

17 *For if by the transgression of the one, death reigned through the one, much more those who receive the abundance of grace and of the gift of righteousness will reign in life through the One, Jesus Christ.*

18 So then as through one transgression there resulted condemnation to all men, even so through one act of righteousness there resulted justification of life to all men.

19 For as through the one man's disobedience the many were made sinners, even so through the obedience of the One the many will be made righteous.

20 The Law came in so that the transgression would increase; but where sin increased, grace abounded all the more,

21 so that, as sin reigned in death, even so grace would reign through righteousness to eternal life through Jesus Christ our Lord.

DISCUSS with your GROUP or PONDER on your own . . .

How did sin enter the world?

How did death enter the world?

Make a simple list of everything you learned by marking *sin* and *death* in the text.

Digging Deeper

Is death just a natural part of life?

Our culture would have us believe that death is simply another part of life, as natural as waking and sleeping, as breathing in and out. Is death just part of the great circle of life or is that just a lie from *The Lyin' King*? If you have some extra time this week, examine the biblical view of death. If you're limited on time, focus on Jesus' view of death and how His mission related to conquering death. Here are a few questions to help you get started.

Was death part of the original creation? Explain your view.

Where is death first mentioned in the Bible? What is the first physical death in the Bible? How are death and sin related?

What was Jesus' view of death? You can consider all four Gospels in full, limit yourself to one or two, or you can narrow your study by running a concordance search on death-related words (*death, dead, die, dying*, etc.). Whatever you decide, though, make sure to read and interact with John 11.

What does Paul teach about death? Again, a concordance will help you locate relevant passages. You don't need to list every fact, simply summarize his overall view.

What does Romans 5:12-21 say about the results of sin that is reminiscent of Romans 8?

ONE STEP FURTHER:

Word Study: Sin

What Hebrew and Greek words are translated "sin"? Where does the English word first appear in the Bible? How are the original Hebrew and Greek words used in Scripture? Run a concordance search and see what you discover. Record your findings below. If you need some extra room, use the margin on page 37.

How does this affect your world view?

If you think people are innately good, what will you expect from them? How can this set you up for disappointment?

If you understand that people are born sinners, how will this impact your thinking and actions?

From all you've read so far, how would you now respond to the statement "Death is just a natural part of life"?

OBSERVE the TEXT of SCRIPTURE

READ Romans 8:18-25 and **CIRCLE** every reference to *creation*. **UNDERLINE** every reference to *waiting eagerly*.

Romans 8:18-25

18 For I consider that the sufferings of this present time are not worthy to be compared with the glory that is to be revealed to us.

19 For the anxious longing of the creation waits eagerly for the revealing of the sons of God.

20 For the creation was subjected to futility, not willingly, but because of Him who subjected it,
in hope

21 that the creation itself also will be set free from its slavery to corruption into the freedom of the glory of the children of God.

22 For we know that the whole creation groans and suffers the pains of childbirth together until now.

23 And not only this, but also we ourselves, having the first fruits of the Spirit, even we ourselves groan within ourselves, waiting eagerly for our adoption as sons, the redemption of our body.

24 For in hope we have been saved, but hope that is seen is not hope; for who hopes for what he already sees?

25 But if we hope for what we do not see, with perseverance we wait eagerly for it.

DISCUSS with your GROUP or PONDER on your own . . .

Look at every reference to *creation* and record what you learned about the condition of creation.

Do the same for *waiting eagerly*. Who is waiting eagerly and for what? Why?

FYI

What It Means differs from *How It Applies* . . .

Every passage of Scripture has one correct interpretation. Let's face it, the author meant to say what he meant to say. So whenever I hear a person say, "This verse means thus-and-so *to me*," I cringe a little. Okay. I cringe A LOT, because the verse has intrinsic meaning.

Application is different. Knowing the correct meaning of one verse, two believers may apply it differently and even multiple ways.

When I consider man's spiritual condition, I extend more patience and compassion in everyday life. I can't say this holds true on greater offenses. It's not an application that can be easily pushed to extremes, at least not for me. But knowing this truth and living in the light of it has changed the way I think and act pretty much every day.

Doesn't sin of all kind provoke God to anger? Yes, sin offends God. We can never forget, though, that as offensive as sin is to God, He reached out to us while we were still His enemies (Romans 5:6-10), He so loved the world that He sent His one and only Son to die on our behalf (John 3:16) and His Spirit produces love, joy, peace, patience, kindness, goodness, faithfulness, gentleness, and self-control (Galatians 5:22-23).

Mindset
Learning and Living the Will of God

An Inductive Study of Romans 8

Did you notice any other key words in this section? If so, what were they and what did you learn from them?

How did the condition of the creation change after the fall?

What implications does this have for how we live?

@THE END OF THE DAY . . .

Take some time to thoroughly reason through the implication of the theological truths we've looked at so far, as well as the implications of believing theological lies. Fill in how you will act based on the truth and also consider what traps lie in wait for those who let lies creep in.

If God is Creator, then . . . .

If I believe the lie that God is not Creator I may . . . .

If I know that all men are sinners, then . . . .

If I believe the lie that people are born basically good or morally neutral I may have problems with . . . .

If I know that death is not part of the created order, then . . . .

If I believe that death is a natural part of the great circle of life . . . .

Living out truth makes all the difference. We'll examine the *how* of this more closely as we talk about walking by faith in the Spirit and setting our minds on God and His ways.

Relax! It's Not Yours to Fix

The Spirit of the Lord GOD is upon me, because the LORD
has anointed me to bring good news to the afflicted;
He has sent me to bind up the brokenhearted,
to proclaim liberty to captives and freedom to prisoners . . .
— Isaiah 61:1

The Law doesn't fix things. Never has. Never will. God's Law is good. It serves a purpose and it is fulfilled in Jesus Christ. It points out the problem but doesn't *solve* it. God fixes the mess mankind started in the garden through the death and resurrection of Jesus Christ. The Law is part of the plan—it shows us the problem, but you and I fulfilling the Law on our own is impossible . . . even for the Type A's among us.

So why do so many of us have an odd love affair with rules and laws and all things "control"? Maybe we don't like to be under laws ourselves, but how often do we impose them on others? Or maybe we like the security of rules, of being able to have a concrete checklist-way to not only obey but also keep records of it! God's Word tells us we are free in Christ Jesus! And yet law-based behavior can creep in stealthily not only to the Church as a whole but also into our lives too.

While it sometimes cleans up nicely and looks good to passers-by, religious bondage is still bondage and Jesus came to set captives free! So this week we're going to look at why what we believe about salvation is so important, not only for our forever-after but also for our here and now!

ONE STEP FURTHER:

Look for Some More about the Law

If you have some extra time this week, run a concordance search and see what you can learn about the law in both the Old and New Testaments. A search will return a bevy of words. Don't get overwhelmed; take some time to start understanding where and how this word is used elsewhere in the Bible.

Record your initial observations below.

Lesson Three: **Relax! It's Not Yours to Fix**

Turning back the clock . . .

We're going to flashback in the text again today to look at where God set us free and how. Before we do that, however, let's start back in Romans 8 to establish our footing and see just how powerless the Law is to fix our situation.

OBSERVE the TEXT of SCRIPTURE

READ Romans 8:1-11 and **CIRCLE** every reference to *law/Law*. Reread the section and color in every instance of *Law* referring to the Law of Moses.

Romans 8:1-11

1   Therefore there is now no condemnation for those who are in Christ Jesus.

2   For the law of the Spirit of life in Christ Jesus has set you free from the law of sin and of death.

3   For what the Law could not do, weak as it was through the flesh, God did: sending His own Son in the likeness of sinful flesh and as an offering *for sin*, He condemned sin in the flesh,

4   so that the requirement of the Law might be fulfilled in us, who do not walk according to the flesh but according to the Spirit.

5   For those who are according to the flesh set their minds on the things of the flesh, but those who are according to the Spirit, the things of the Spirit.

6   For the mind set on the flesh is death, but the mind set on the Spirit is life and peace,

7   because the mind set on the flesh is hostile toward God; for it does not subject itself to the law of God, for it is not even able to do so,

8   and those who are in the flesh cannot please God.

9   However, you are not in the flesh but in the Spirit, if indeed the Spirit of God dwells in you. But if anyone does not have the Spirit of Christ, he does not belong to Him.

10 If Christ is in you, though the body is dead because of sin, yet the spirit is alive because of righteousness.

11 But if the Spirit of Him who raised Jesus from the dead dwells in you, He who raised Christ Jesus from the dead will also give life to your mortal bodies through His Spirit who dwells in you.

FYI:

A Schoolmaster to Lead us to Christ

21 Is the Law then contrary to the promises of God? May it never be! For if a law had been given which was able to impart life, then righteousness would indeed have been based on law.

22 But the Scripture has shut up everyone under sin, so that the promise by faith in Jesus Christ might be given to those who believe.

23 But before faith came, we were kept in custody under the law, being shut up to the faith which was later to be revealed.

24 Therefore the Law has become our tutor *to lead us* to Christ, so that we may be justified by faith.

25 But now that faith has come, we are no longer under a tutor.

—Galatians 3:21-25

DISCUSS with your GROUP or PONDER on your own . . .

What was the Law of Moses powerless to do?

How did God set us free from the law of sin and of death?

If the law brings sin and death, is it bad? Defend your answer. Don't overlook the word *dikaioma* (translated *requirement* by the NASB) in verse 4 as you respond.

How is the requirement of the Law fulfilled in us? If we are free from the law of sin and death, how do we subject ourselves to God today? What "law" do we operate under and how is it different from the other laws?

Paul tells us that "what the Law could not do . . . God did" by sending Jesus. We're going to pick up our next text from the Gospel of John where we see Jesus talking with Nicodemus, a Jewish ruler, about the need to be born again. Remember, we've already seen that sin has brought death to mankind, but Jesus explains a new birth to Nicodemus. The world was broken at the fall, but God will not leave it that way forever.

ONE STEP FURTHER:

Could not, cannot, not even able . . .

If you have some extra time this week, see what you can unearth about the common root in the following italicized phrases:

Romans 8:3 — For what the Law *could not do . . .*

Romans 8:7 — . . . the mind set on the flesh . . . is *not even able . . .*

Romans 8:8 — . . . those who are in the flesh *cannot* please God.

Record your observations below.

Mindset

Learning and Living the Will of God

An Inductive Study of Romans 8

OBSERVE the TEXT of SCRIPTURE

READ John 3:1-21 and **CIRCLE** every reference to *born* or *born again*. **UNDERLINE** every reference to *believe*.

John 3:1-21

1   Now there was a man of the Pharisees, named Nicodemus, a ruler of the Jews;

2   this man came to Jesus by night and said to Him, "Rabbi, we know that You have come from God as a teacher; for no one can do these signs that You do unless God is with him."

3   Jesus answered and said to him, "Truly, truly, I say to you, unless one is born again he cannot see the kingdom of God."

4   Nicodemus said to Him, "How can a man be born when he is old? He cannot enter a second time into his mother's womb and be born, can he?"

5   Jesus answered, "Truly, truly, I say to you, unless one is born of water and the Spirit he cannot enter into the kingdom of God.

6   "That which is born of the flesh is flesh, and that which is born of the Spirit is spirit.

7   "Do not be amazed that I said to you, 'You must be born again.'

8   "The wind blows where it wishes and you hear the sound of it, but do not know where it comes from and where it is going; so is everyone who is born of the Spirit."

9   Nicodemus said to Him, "How can these things be?"

10 Jesus answered and said to him, "Are you the teacher of Israel and do not understand these things?

11 "Truly, truly, I say to you, we speak of what we know and testify of what we have seen, and you do not accept our testimony.

12 "If I told you earthly things and you do not believe, how will you believe if I tell you heavenly things?

13 "No one has ascended into heaven, but He who descended from heaven: the Son of Man.

14 "As Moses lifted up the serpent in the wilderness, even so must the Son of Man be lifted up;

15 so that whoever believes will in Him have eternal life.

16 "For God so loved the world, that He gave His only begotten Son, that whoever believes in Him shall not perish, but have eternal life.

17 "For God did not send the Son into the world to judge the world, but that the world might be saved through Him.

18 "He who believes in Him is not judged; he who does not believe has been judged already, because he has not believed in the name of the only begotten Son of God.

19 "This is the judgment, that the Light has come into the world, and men loved the darkness rather than the Light, for their deeds were evil.

ONE STEP FURTHER:

Word Study: Born Again

Where else does the phrase *born again* appear in the Bible? Use your concordance to find out. What do their contexts tell you? Which writer uses the phase? What do you learn from the other occurrences?

Record your findings below.

---

20 *"For everyone who does evil hates the Light, and does not come to the Light for fear that his deeds will be exposed.*

21 *"But he who practices the truth comes to the Light, so that his deeds may be manifested as having been wrought in God."*

DISCUSS with your GROUP or PONDER on your own . . .

What statement does Jesus open up with?

What did you learn from marking *born* and *born again*?

What is necessary to enter the kingdom of God? From what you know already about creation and the fall of mankind, does this make sense to you?

What other key words did you notice? What did you learn by marking them?

Learning and Living the Will of God

An Inductive Study of Romans 8

Why did God send His Son into the world?

Notes

FYI:

Sin Causes People to Hide

9 Then the LORD God called to the man, and said to him, "Where are you?"

10 He said, "I heard the sound of You in the garden, and I was afraid because I was naked; so I hid myself."

11 And He said, "Who told you that you were naked? Have you eaten from the tree of which I commanded you not to eat?"

—Genesis 3:9-11

Do you know people who are hiding today? Are you hiding? How can the truth set captives free?

Did you mark words associated with judgment in this section? If so, what did you observe?

What is the condition of those who don't believe?

One more time, just so we're clear: Why did Jesus come into the world?

How do those who do evil treat the Light according to Jesus? Does this remind you of anything in the early chapters of Genesis? If so, what?

How can we minister to people whose sin causes them to hide?

What about us? How can knowing this change the way we deal with sin in our own lives? Explain.

Before we move on, we need to consider another area of application of utmost importance. What are we doing about those who are under judgment for loving darkness rather than light? Are you showing God's love to people who don't know Jesus? If so, how? If not, how can you?

Do you share the good news of Jesus with people who are living in darkness? Explain.

Who did God use to bring you to Jesus? Is there anything you can learn from your conversion that can inform your attitude and behavior as you share the Gospel with others?

Before you turn the page, ask God if there is a specific person in your life you should be talking to about Jesus. Record your thoughts below.

ONE STEP FURTHER:

Word Study: Continue

If you have some time this week, see what you can find out about the word translated *continue* in John 8:31. See where else it is used and how, paying close attention to how John uses it elsewhere in this Gospel and in his letters. Record your findings below.

Digging Deeper

Investigate Galatians

The letter to the Galatians is often referred to as a mini-Romans. This makes it of special interest to us as we study Romans 8. Paul addresses many of the same issues in both letters. If you're up for some extra study this week, read through the letter to the Galatians. I'll get you started with some questions below, but always be asking the 5W and H questions for yourself as you read.

What is the main problem Paul addresses to the church at Galatia?

Who is involved?

Why does Paul consider it such a big deal?

How does Paul contrast the life lived in the flesh versus the life lived in the Spirit?

Spend some time with God asking Him to hold your life up to the plumbline in Galatians to see if you are walking by the flesh or walking by the Spirit. As you do, remember that the church at Galatia was trying to pursue spiritual ends by means of the flesh. This a common problem. Ask God to help you see clearly if you need a course correction. Jot below things you need to remember.

FYI

The Verse that Hit Me Between the Eyes

We all have our own stuff. Part of mine is double type-A perfectionism and drive. It's not pretty. (I know, at this point you're either totally relating with me or totally laughing at me! I'm okay with either.) Part of the uglier side of what's already rather grim to start with is the draw to goals, benchmarks, and measurements to prove to myself "how good" *I'm* doing.

I have never had a problem with the truth that I am saved by grace through faith and that there is nothing I can do to work my way to God. On that I have always been pretty crystal clear. The lie that grabs at me, though, is that I have to do the job of sanctification on my own—the lie that God saves me, but I behaves me.

The truth of Galatians 3:3 has been life-giving to me, as I learn more and more to relax in the truth that what God has begun in me by the Spirit, He is also perfecting by the Spirit!

Having begun by the Spirit, are you now being perfected by the flesh?
—Galatians 3:3b

Lesson Three: **Relax! It's Not Yours to Fix**

Recapping the situation . . .

Since the fall, mankind has been in bad, bad shape—separated from God, under condemnation, and held in bondage to sin and death. Everyone starts out mired in this condition, but Jesus came to set us free! Let's look at some more of His words regarding this freedom.

OBSERVE the TEXT of SCRIPTURE

READ John 8:31-36 and **CIRCLE** every occurrence of *free*. **UNDERLINE** every reference to *slavery* (*slave, enslaved*, etc.). **BOX** every reference to *truth*.

John 8:31-36

31 *So Jesus was saying to those Jews who had believed Him, "If you continue in My word,* then *you are truly disciples of Mine;*

32 *and you will know the truth, and the truth will make you free."*

33 *They answered Him, "We are Abraham's descendants and have never yet been enslaved to anyone; how is it that You say, 'You will become free'?"*

34 *Jesus answered them, "Truly, truly, I say to you, everyone who commits sin is the slave of sin.*

35 *"The slave does not remain in the house forever; the son does remain forever.*

36 *"So if the Son makes you free, you will be free indeed.*

DISCUSS with your GROUP or PONDER on your own . . .

Make a simple list of everything you learned from marking *free*. What was your most interesting finding?

Now make a simple list of everything you learned from marking *slave/enslaved*.

Who is a slave?

How does a person become free?

Are you living today as a slave to sin or in the freedom Jesus has provided? Why?

What role does truth (the Word) p ay in freedom?

What application can you make from this passage to your life this week?

Where is the power?

Although it runs counter to everything in us that wants to work and achieve and save ourselves, Scripture is clear that God saves us. In Romans 6 we see that the power to live God's way comes not from intestinal fortitude but from being united with Christ.

OBSERVE the TEXT of SCRIPTURE

READ Romans 6 and consider how God has freed us from sin through the death and resurrection of Jesus Christ. **CIRCLE** every reference to *death (death, died, dead, crucified)*, **UNDERLINE** *slavery* and **BOX** *sin*.

Romans 6

1   What shall we say then? Are we to continue in sin so that grace may increase?

2   May it never be! How shall we who died to sin still live in it?

3   Or do you not know that all of us who have been baptized into Christ Jesus have been baptized into His death?

4   Therefore we have been buried with Him through baptism into death, so that as Christ was raised from the dead through the glory of the Father, so we too might walk in newness of life.

5   For if we have become united with Him in the likeness of His death, certainly we shall also be in the likeness of His resurrection,

6   knowing this, that our old self was crucified with Him, in order that our body of sin might be done away with, so that we would no longer be slaves to sin;

7   for he who has died is freed from sin.

8   Now if we have died with Christ, we believe that we shall also live with Him,

9   knowing that Christ, having been raised from the dead, is never to die again; death no longer is master over Him.

10   For the death that He died, He died to sin once for all; but the life that He lives, He lives to God.

11   Even so consider yourselves to be dead to sin, but alive to God in Christ Jesus.

12   Therefore do not let sin reign in your mortal body so that you obey its lusts,

13   and do not go on presenting the members of your body to sin as instruments of unrighteousness; but present yourselves to God as those alive from the dead, and your members as instruments of righteousness to God.

14   For sin shall not be master over you, for you are not under law but under grace.

15   What then? Shall we sin because we are not under law but under grace? May it never be!

16   Do you not know that when you present yourselves to someone as slaves for obedience, you are slaves of the one whom you obey, either of sin resulting in death, or of obedience resulting in righteousness?

FYI:

Shall we continue in sin to get more grace?

Paul begins Romans 6 alluding to a heresy that had been circulating. Church historians named it **Antinomianism** because it was against (anti-) law *(nomos)*. The idea is that you throw the law out the window and sin more to receive more grace, more *unconditional* love. Clearly this runs counter to Paul's teaching. We don't sin in order to get more grace. Rather, through the Spirit—not the Law—God empowers us to live as instruments of righteousness.

17 But thanks be to God that though you were slaves of sin, you became obedient from the heart to that form of teaching to which you were committed,

18 and having been freed from sin, you became slaves of righteousness.

19 I am speaking in human terms because of the weakness of your flesh. For just as you presented your members as slaves to impurity and to lawlessness, resulting in further lawlessness, so now present your members as slaves to righteousness, resulting in sanctification.

20 For when you were slaves of sin, you were free in regard to righteousness.

21 Therefore what benefit were you then deriving from the things of which you are now ashamed? For the outcome of those things is death.

22 But now having been freed from sin and enslaved to God, you derive your benefit, resulting in sanctification, and the outcome, eternal life.

23 For the wages of sin is death, but the free gift of God is eternal life in Christ Jesus our Lord.

DISCUSS with your GROUP or PONDER on your own . . .

We marked *death*, *slavery*, and *sin*. Do you see another set of contrasting words in the text you can mark?

What is Paul's basic argument in this section? What power works in our life before salvation? What power works now?

ONE STEP FURTHER:

Antinomianism Refuted

Anyone drawn to the antinomian heresy need only read the words of Jesus in the Sermon on the Mount. If you have some time this week, read what Jesus has to say in Matthew 5:13-20 and then record your observations below.

Mindset
Learning and Living the Will of God

An Inductive Study of Romans 8

What does Jesus' death on the cross have to do with us?

According to verse 14, what is true of all those not under the law but under grace?

What characterizes the life "under grace"?

OBSERVE the TEXT of SCRIPTURE

In the book of Galatians, Paul confronts leaders who teach that believers must keep Jewish laws, including circumcision, in order to be saved.

READ Galatians 3:1-3 and **MARK** the key words.

Galatians 3:1-3

1   You foolish Galatians, who has bewitched you, before whose eyes Jesus Christ was publicly portrayed as crucified?

2   This is the only thing I want to find out from you: did you receive the Spirit by the works of the Law, or by hearing with faith?

3   Are you so foolish? Having begun by the Spirit, are you now being perfected by the flesh?

DISCUSS with your GROUP or PONDER on your own . . .

What words and phrases did you mark as being "key" to this section? Explain your choice(s).

How did the Galatians receive the Spirit?

How does Paul imply they are trying to follow God now?

Do people today try to follow God on their own power in ways similar to the ways the Galatians were doing? What are some current day examples?

Are there any ways you are trying to be "perfected by the flesh"?

Are there ways you try to cause others to be "perfected by the flesh"?

ONE STEP FURTHER:

Word Study: Perfected

If you have some time this week, see what Greek word is behind "perfected." Don't forget to examine how it is used elsewhere before you break out word study materials. Record your observations below.

OBSERVE the TEXT of SCRIPTURE

READ Galatians 5:1-16 and **CIRCLE** every reference to *freedom (free, freedom)*. Again, **WATCH** the contrasts between *law* and *grace, slavery* and *freedom, flesh* and *Spirit*.

Galatians 5:1-16

1   It was for freedom that Christ set us free; therefore keep standing firm and do not be subject again to a yoke of slavery.

2   Behold I, Paul, say to you that if you receive circumcision, Christ will be of no benefit to you.

3   And I testify again to every man who receives circumcision, that he is under obligation to keep the whole Law.

4   You have been severed from Christ, you who are seeking to be justified by law; you have fallen from grace.

5   For we through the Spirit, by faith, are awaiting for the hope of righteousness.

6   For in Christ Jesus neither circumcision nor uncircumcision means anything, but faith working through love.

7   You were running well; who hindered you from obeying the truth?

8   This persuasion did not come from Him who calls you.

9   A little leaven leavens the whole lump of dough.

10   I have confidence in you in the Lord that you will adopt no other view; but the one who is disturbing you will bear his judgment, whoever he is.

11   But I, brethren, if I still preach circumcision, why am I still persecuted? Then the stumbling block of the cross has been abolished.

12   I wish that those who are troubling you would even mutilate themselves.

13   For you were called to freedom, brethren; only do not turn your freedom into an opportunity for the flesh, but through love serve one another.

14   For the whole Law is fulfilled in one word, in the statement, "YOU SHALL LOVE YOUR NEIGHBOR AS YOURSELF."

15   But if you bite and devour one another, take care that you are not consumed by one another.

16   But I say, walk by the Spirit, and you will not carry out the desire of the flesh.

FYI:

The Historical Context of Galatians

If you're new to reading the Bible, the discussion on circumcision may seem straight out of left field. Here's a bit of context. Jews in Galatia were trying to cause Gentile believers to go beyond justification by faith alone in the atonement accomplished by the death and resurrection of Jesus Christ. They taught that compliance with Moses' Law, including circumcision, was necessary for salvation. In doing so they were adding to the finished work of Christ and trying to bring free men back to a different form of slavery (cf. Romans 6:20-22). But remember what we said when we started our study? Religious slavery may clean up the outside but it can't clean the inside that remains enslaved; and slavery is slavery!

DISCUSS with your GROUP or PONDER on your own . . .

What contrasts does Paul bring out in this passage? Are they mutually exclusive or inclusive? Give some examples and note how you can apply them when you're talking to someone about salvation.

What does Paul say about freedom in this section?

According to verse 13, what are believers not to do with their freedom?

How is the Law fulfilled by those who are free?

What is the key to not acting in the flesh?

The Galatians were threatened by the teaching that circumcision was necessary for salvation. Are you adding to faith in Christ to try and make yourself and or others better in God's eyes?

ONE STEP FURTHER:

Word Study: Free/Freedom

If you have some extra time, look into the Greek and Hebrew words behind *free* and *freedom*. See where and how they are used elsewhere in the Bible. Here are a few questions to get you started: *What brings freedom? What takes it away? What characterizes freedom?* Record your observations below.

Mindset
Learning and Living the Will of God
An Inductive Study of Romans 8

Digging Deeper

Predestination and Free Will

Next week we are going to look at little closer at the concepts of predestination and free will in the main portion of our lesson. I'll point you to some places where we see both God's sovereignty and man's free will attested to in Scripture.

If you're up for the challenge, though, I'd love for you to jump in and see how far you can get navigating these waters on your own first. Run some concordance searches from Romans 8 and see where the texts take you. Look for terms in Romans 8:28-30 to get you started.

What does God's Word say about God's sovereignty in salvation?

Soteriology

This big word means the study of salvation. You've been engaging in soteriology all week.

What does God's Word say about man's choice?

How do we live in light of both of these truths?

OBSERVE the TEXT of SCRIPTURE

READ Hebrews 10:1-14 and **MARK** every reference to *sacrifices* and *offerings* (including pronouns). Also **WATCH** for what the *Law* can and cannot do.

Hebrews 10:1-14

1   For the Law, since it has only *a shadow of the good things to come* and *not the very form of things, can never, by the same sacrifices which they offer continually year by year, make perfect those who draw near.*

2   Otherwise, would they not have ceased to be offered, because the worshipers, having once been cleansed, would no longer have had consciousness of sins?

3   But in those sacrifices *there is a reminder of sins year by year.*

4   For it is impossible for the blood of bulls and goats to take away sins.

5   Therefore, when He comes into the world, He says,

"SACRIFICE AND OFFERING YOU HAVE NOT DESIRED,

BUT A BODY YOU HAVE PREPARED FOR ME;

6   IN WHOLE BURNT OFFERINGS AND sacrifices FOR SIN YOU HAVE TAKEN NO PLEASURE.

7   "THEN I SAID, 'BEHOLD, I HAVE COME

(IN THE SCROLL OF THE BOOK IT IS WRITTEN OF ME)

TO DO YOUR WILL, O GOD.' "

8   After saying above, "SACRIFICES AND OFFERINGS AND WHOLE BURNT OFFERINGS AND sacrifices FOR SIN YOU HAVE NOT DESIRED, NOR HAVE YOU TAKEN PLEASURE in them" *(which are offered according to the Law),*

9   then He said, "BEHOLD, I HAVE COME TO DO YOUR WILL." He takes away the first in order to establish the second.

10 By this will we have been sanctified through the offering of the body of Jesus Christ once for all.

11 Every priest stands daily ministering and offering time after time the same sacrifices, which   can never take away sins;

12 but He, having offered one sacrifice for sins for all time, SAT DOWN AT THE RIGHT HAND   OF GOD,

13 waiting from that time onward UNTIL HIS ENEMIES BE MADE A FOOTSTOOL FOR HIS FEET.

14 For by one offering He has perfected for all time those who are sanctified.

DISCUSS with your GROUP or PONDER on your own . . .

What did you learn in this passage about what the Law specifically can and cannot do?

What about sacrifices offered under the Law? How do they differ from the sacrifice of Jesus?

What did the sacrifice of Jesus do for those who belong to Him? Be specific.

How will these truths affect you this week? For instance, how will you live knowing your sins are not just covered but also taken away? Go through and consider specific applications of the benefits you recorded above.

Spend Some Time in Leviticus

When we read about sacrifices in the book of Hebrews, we're given only a glimpse of what the sacrificial system looked like. If you have some time on your hands this week, invest a little of it in scanning through the rules and regulations in the book of Leviticus and record some basic observations below.

Mindset

Learning and Living the Will of God

An Inductive Study of Romans 8

@THE END OF THE DAY . . .

Soteriology, the doctrine of salvation, matters! Understanding fully that we can't save or sanctify ourselves should change the way we live and interact with others. Only God can save, only God can sanctify. We submit, but He saves us and grows us.

Do I wish I could make myself grow spiritually? Do I wish I could make others grow spiritually? Yeah! But I can't. It is a work of the Spirit and He is powerful enough to do it without my controlling oversight. I am, though, called to witness to the Gospel and to encourage others in the faith.

As we wrap up this week of study, take some time to be still before God and ask Him if there are any ways you are adding to His free gift with works of the flesh. Consider one truth you learned this week that is more applicable in your life right now than any others. Record it below and ask God how you can most effectively begin living it out hour by hour.

Finally, before our next time together, write out your testimony of faith and ask God how you can live with more intentionality. How can you make God's mission to reach lost people more of a priority in your life? Who will you pray for? How will you show God's love to those around you? Who will you talk to about what Jesus has done for you?

Notes

The Perfect Father and the End of Dysfunction

For you have not received a spirit of slavery leading to fear again,
but you have received a spirit of adoption as sons
by which we cry out, "Abba! Father!"
—Romans 8:15

If you are in relationship with Jesus Christ, it is because God adopted you. I know. It's too simple. But it's what He tells us in His Word. We were separated from Him, we stood condemned, we were outside the family and He adopted us into the family. It's a basic metaphor people can understand and yet we still get ourselves confused from time to time. Have you ever noticed that sometimes instead of simply receiving the adoption and accepting God's gracious gift we wear ourselves out trying to "*make* God's team"?

This week we're going to continue looking at the doctrine of salvation as we jump back into Romans 8:12-17 and 28-30. We'll discover firsthand what the Word teaches about how God went about saving and adopting the likes of us and we'll wrestle with what difference this truth makes . . .
or should make!

Are you living like a son or daughter of the King of kings . . . or are you still living like a slave? That is the question at hand!

ONE STEP FURTHER:

Word Study: Adoption
Take some time this week and find the compound Greek word translated as *adoption*. This word, which is entirely Pauline, appears in the following New Testament passages and is absent from the LXX (the Septuagint, the Greek translation of the Old Testament). See what you discover in each of these verses before consulting any commentaries or word study helps.

Romans 8:15

Romans 8:23

Romans 9:4

Galatians 4:5

Ephesians 1:5

General observations:

Mindset
Learning and Living the Will of God

An Inductive Study of Romans 8

AN OVERVIEW OF THE TEXT
OBSERVE the TEXT of SCRIPTURE

READ Romans 8:12-17 and **MARK** all family-related words (*sons, adoption, Father,* etc.). You can **MARK** the word group in the same way or choose more specific markings for the individual words.

Romans 8:12-17

12 So then, brethren, we are under obligation, not to the flesh, to live according to the flesh—

13 for if you are living according to the flesh, you must die; but if by the Spirit you are putting to death the deeds of the body, you will live.

14 For all who are being led by the Spirit of God, these are sons of God.

15 For you have not received a spirit of slavery leading to fear again, but you have received a spirit of adoption as sons by which we cry out, "Abba! Father!"

16 The Spirit Himself testifies with our spirit that we are children of God,

17 and if children, heirs also, heirs of God and fellow heirs with Christ, if indeed we suffer with Him so that we may also be glorified with Him.

DISCUSS with your GROUP or PONDER on your own . . .

What relationship has God brought us into?

What evidences this relationship?

Mindset
Learning and Living the Will of God

An Inductive Study of Romans 8

What does the spirit of slavery lead to?

What benefits come with sonship?

What else comes with being a fellow heir?

Let's get practical here: do you earn adoption? Can you work for sonship? Explain.

If you know you are accepted, how does that change your outlook? How does it change your behavior?

FYI:

. . . and the Peace that Follows

Whenever possible I'd arrive early to ballgames in the hope of snagging even a batting practice cast-off. Year after year, though, I snagged nothing but disappointment. Every moment in a ball park, regardless of how much fun I was having, was filled with a bit of angst as I was always on the prowl for a ball. As hard as I was trying, I never knew if I'd end up in the club. Last summer everything changed when I caught my first ball at Safeco Field in Seattle. Strangely enough, within the next 24 hours I had two more and about a month later we got yet another at Miller Park in Milwaukee.

Stick with me here. Something changed after the first ball was in my hand and then in my purse. I had what I was after and I relaxed. I still love chasing base-balls, but now it is angst-free. I'm "in the club" . . . I'm in the family of people who already have a baseball . . I no longer need to get there.

This may not make sense to you, but the change in my outlook made me think of the difference between resting and striving in my life with Christ. Getting the ball didn't change my zeal to chase baseballs; it hasn't made me lazy by any means. Knowing I have one, though, has changed my heart. Now I can relax and enjoy the game! How often over the years have I run around with angst in my spiritual life, in a sense trying to get what God has already so graciously given to me in Christ!

Learning and Living the Will of God

An Inductive Study of Romans 8

OBSERVE the TEXT of SCRIPTURE

Let's take a closer look at what Paul has to say about adoption in Galatians.

READ Galatians 4:1-9 and **CIRCLE** every *child/son* reference (*child, son, children, heir,* and pronouns). **UNDERLINE** every reference to *God* (include synonyms and pronouns).

Galatians 4:1-9

1   *Now I say, as long as the heir is a child, he does not differ at all from a slave although he is owner of everything,*

2   *but he is under guardians and managers until the date set by the father.*

3   *So also we, while we were children, were held in bondage under the elemental things of the world.*

4   *But when the fullness of the time came, God sent forth His Son, born of a woman, born under the Law,*

5   *so that He might redeem those who were under the Law, that we might receive the adoption as sons.*

6   *Because you are sons, God has sent forth the Spirit of His Son into our hearts, crying, "Abba! Father!"*

7   *Therefore you are no longer a slave, but a son; and if a son, then an heir through God.*

8   *However at that time, when you did not know God, you were slaves to those which by nature are no gods.*

9   *But now that you have come to know God, or rather to be known by God, how is it that you turn back again to the weak and worthless elemental things, to which you desire to be enslaved all over again?*

DISCUSS with your GROUP or PONDER on your own . . .

What did you learn by marking references to sonship?

According to verse 6, what has God sent forth into our hearts? What difference does this make?

Abba

In Romans 8, Galatians 4 and Mark 14:36 we see the use of Abba in reference to God. This is a very intimate term, essentially Aramaic for *Daddy*.

Aramaic, like Hebrew, is a Semitic language and is probably the one Jesus and his disciples used in their everyday interactions.

Assuming You are Accepted

I have a friend who explains that every time she enters a room she assumes people like her until they prove her wrong. You know what? Thinking you're already accepted versus trying to work for people's approval changes the whole way you go about things. We may know that we're saved by faith and that living the life God calls us to is a result of His saving us, but if we don't fully grasp that acceptance and the completed work of Jesus, we will fall back into striving behavior—behavior that acts out of a need *for* acceptance, as opposed to living a passionate life *of* acceptance. We can confidently live like we're accepted by God, because through Jesus, we are!

What did you learn about God?

What other word or words in this section will you look at more closely? Why?

READ through Galatians 4:1-10 again and **MARK** references to time or time phrases. Then record what you learn from marking them. What was our condition before Christ? What is the condition now of those who have been redeemed?

What was Paul's concern in this passage? How were the Galatians behaving?

What characterizes slavery? Be sure to include references for your answers and feel free to include answers from other parts of Scripture.

INDUCTIVE FOCUS:

The Importance of Time Phrases

Observing and marking time phrases in the text is an important part of the inductive process. You can draw a clock by the word or phrase, pick a specific color to use consistently for time, or something else. Just choose a method and stick with it.

Paying attention to time phrases helps us interpret the text because these words and phrases give us loads of information on when things happened (or will happen) and their sequence.

Some of the words and phrases you'll catch in Galatians 4:1-9 are *when, as long as, until, no longer,* and *now.*

Mindset
Learning and Living the Will of God
An Inductive Study of Romans 8

Consider your life carefully. What behaviors characterize you? Do you live as a son or a slave? What specific behaviors or ways of thinking support your view?

OBSERVE the TEXT of SCRIPTURE

As we look at another passage dealing with sonship, we'll pick up a touchy topic associated with it in Romans 8, predestination. Chances are you already have an opinion. Remember, we're looking to God's Word not to preconceived ideas we have. So as we proceed let's continue to trust God and let Him speak for Himself through His Word.

READ Ephesians 1:3-14 and **UNDERLINE** every time the phrase *in Christ* (or a synonym) appears. **MARK** every reference to God's *purpose* and/or *intention*. Don't forget to keep your eyes open for time phrases. There are some whoppers in this passage.

Ephesians 1:3-14

3   Blessed be the God and Father of our Lord Jesus Christ, who has blessed us with every spiritual blessing in the heavenly places in Christ,

4   just as He chose us in Him before the foundation of the world, that we would be holy and blameless before Him. In love

5   He predestined us to adoption as sons through Jesus Christ to Himself, according to the kind intention of His will,

6   to the praise of the glory of His grace, which He freely bestowed on us in the Beloved.

7   In Him we have redemption through His blood, the forgiveness of our trespasses, according to the riches of His grace

8   which He lavished on us. In all wisdom and insight

9   He made known to us the mystery of His will, according to His kind intention which He purposed in Him

10   with a view to an administration suitable to the fullness of the times, that is, the summing up of all things in Christ, things in the heavens and things on the earth. In Him

11   also we have obtained an inheritance, having been predestined according to His purpose who works all things after the counsel of His will,

12   to the end that we who were the first to hope in Christ would be to the praise of His glory.

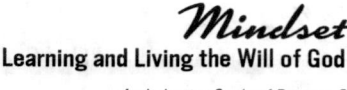

13 *In Him, you also, after listening to the message of truth, the gospel of your salvation—having also believed, you were sealed in Him with the Holy Spirit of promise,*

14 *who is given as a pledge of our inheritance, with a view to the redemption of God's own possession, to the praise of His glory.*

DISCUSS with your GROUP or PONDER on your own . . .

How many times does the phrase *in Christ* (or *in Him*) appear in this section? How is it related to everything else?

According to verse 5, what did God predestine us to? Why?

When did He choose us? Given the timing, is there anything we could have done to earn this "draft pick" to "make the team"?

What actions did God take toward us? Let me start you off . . . He *blessed* us (verse 3), He *chose* us (verse 4) . . .

ONE STEP FURTHER:

Word Studies

If you have some time, see what you can discover about the key verbs in Romans 8:29-30. See what you can find out about the tense of the verbs in this passage and also how the verbs are used elsewhere.

Foreknew

Predestined

Called

Justified

Glorified

Mindset
Learning and Living the Will of God
An Inductive Study of Romans 8

What does the text tell us about sonship?

How and where does Paul refer to God's action in predestination? What specifically does he say?

What do we learn about God's plan? Does He have one? Does He have things under control?

Do you live like you believe God has a plan?

Let's get a little more specific. Are you harboring worry over a life situation that would disappear if you knew beyond a shadow of a doubt that God had your back? If so, write it down and talk to Him about it.

Does the idea of predestination bother you? We need to remember the Bible repeatedly says that God is good. His Word teaches that He makes choices and so does every man. There's some mystery in this but we can trust Him to sort things out later, if not right now. We take what is clear in Scripture (which is plenty) and we trust God with the rest.

FYI:

Predestined

Though the historical theological systems known as Calvinism and Arminianism both affirm predestination, they interpret it differently.

The basic views:

Calvinists believe God chooses based on His mercy alone, apart from anything the person will do.

Arminians believe God chooses based on knowing what people will do (choose, believe, work, persevere, etc.).

While there are subsets of both Calvinism and Arminianism, as well as a few other spins on the subject, we need to affirm what the Bible says.

Digging Deeper

So what is the "will" of God?

We've come across quite a few "God's will" words already this week: *will, purpose, kind intention.* What does God's Word say about God's will?

Before you start digging, let's think about the questions people ask. What questions have you heard people ask regarding God's will?

What questions do you find yourself asking?

Who is at the center of your questions, you or God? Are you more concerned with His purposes or His specific plans for you? Explain.

Consider this concept first in Romans 8, next in Romans, then in Paul's other writings and out from there. Record what you discover about God's will in each section and how we should respond.

Romans 8:

What's the plan?

Ever had a kid who needs to know "The Plan" and gets out of sorts if he doesn't? My oldest is very easygoing and agreeable as long as he knows what's coming. He doesn't care what the plan is nearly as much as "getting the memo." There are days he comes close to making me crazy with continual "What's the plan?" interrogations. *Does he not trust me? Can he not give me the slightest benefit of the doubt that I have his good in mind even when I'm asking him to trust me with the details? Doesn't he understand that I have not only his back but also his best interests in mind?*

When I sit back and think about it, he's "with me" the way I've been "with God" over the years. Trusting that He is good and does good can make all the difference in how we live from day to day.

Romans:

Paul's other writings:

Other New Testament writings:

Old Testament view:

Based on everything you're discovered this week, what is your biggest application point regarding the will of God?

OBSERVE the TEXT of SCRIPTURE

In this section we're going to focus on verses 28-30. We'll circle back to the others later when we talk about prayer and talk further about God's will (so don't worry, we're not skipping them!), but for now we will look at them as context for the other verses.

READ Romans 8:26-34. In Romans 8:28-30, **MARK** every reference to God (include pronouns—you can mark with a triangle or some other way). **MARK** every reference to the Son (again, include pronouns and mark with a cross, a different color, or something else memorable). Finally, **CIRCLE** every reference to "those who love God" including pronouns.

Romans 8:26-34

26 *In the same way the Spirit also helps our weakness; for we do not know how to pray as we should, but the Spirit Himself intercedes for us with groanings too deep for words;*

27 *and He who searches the hearts knows what the mind of the Spirit is, because He intercedes for the saints according to the will of God.*

28 *And we know that God causes all things to work together for good to those who love God, to those who are called according to His purpose.*

29 *For those whom He foreknew, He also predestined to become conformed to the image of His Son, so that He would be the firstborn among many brethren;*

30 *and these whom He predestined, He also called; and these whom He called, He also justified; and these whom He justified, He also glorified.*

31 *What then shall we say to these things? If God is for us, who is against us?*

32 *He who did not spare His own Son, but delivered Him over for us all, how will He not also with Him freely give us all things?*

33 *Who will bring a charge against God's elect? God is the one who justifies;*

34 *who is the one who condemns? Christ Jesus is He who died, yes, rather who was raised, who is at the right hand of God, who also intercedes for us.*

DISCUSS with your GROUP or PONDER on your own . . .

What does God do in verses 28-30?

Learning and Living the Will of God

An Inductive Study of Romans 8

What series of actions are laid out in verses 29-30?

What are the tenses of the verbs?

Did those foreknown, predestined, called, etc. do something to merit these actions?

Consider verse 28 for a moment. Which came first, God's call or man's love? Reason from the text and support your answer with other scriptures.

What life-anchoring truth does Paul present in Romans 8:28?

For whom do all things work together for good? (Make sure you get the whole answer!)

Does this mean all "things" themselves are good? Explain.

What can we learn about God's purpose from this text?

Since we've been chatting predestination, what does this text say about predestination? What is the objective goal of predestination here?

What else do we know about *image* biblically?

ONE STEP FURTHER:

Word Study: Work Together

If you have some extra time this week, see what you can find out about the Greek word that translates *work together* in Romans 8:28. Record your findings below.

How can living by the truth of Romans 8:28 radically change a person's perspective when facing hard times? Think, pray, and record some specifics.

What assurance do God's actions in Romans 8:29-30 give us? How can these truths help us combat doubt about the future?

Does God call people to Himself? The biblical answer is a definite "Yes." So how can people have free will if God is sovereign? I don't know—He just hasn't revealed everything . . . yet. There are "secret things" that belong only to Him (Deuteronomy 29:29). The Bible clearly teaches both sovereignty and responsibility. I can't define how the two harmonize, but I know that it is not a problem for God. I also can't explain the details of how a rocket can travel to the moon, but my lack of knowledge does not make the reality any less true. What I do know, though, is this: Because God is sovereign, I can have peace and I can rest.

Before we finish off our time this week, let's look at the other side of the coin and consider some passages of Scripture that show the outstretched arms of our missionary God to all people.

Digging Deeper

Why the difference in translations?

Sometimes in reading different Bible translations we notice simple stylistic differences, other times we notice content differences. In Romans 8:28, the big translation question that surfaces is "What is the subject of the verb translated *work(s) together?*"

If you have some time this week, take a look at the ways the following renderings differ from one another and consider if these differences in translation affect meaning and application. In each instance I've highlighted the word or phrase translated as the subject. In the *ESV and KJV* the translators have *all things working together.* The *NASB* and *NIV* have *God causing all things to work together.* Note the differences in the texts below:

*ESV | Ro 8:28 And we know that for those who love God **all things** work together for good, for those who are called according to his purpose.*

*KJV | Ro 8:28 And we know that **all things** work together for good to them that love God, to them who are the called according to his purpose.*

*NASB95 | Ro 8:28 And we know that **God** causes all things to work together for good to those who love God, to those who are called according to His purpose.*

*NIV | Ro 8:28 And we know that in all things **God** works for the good of those who love him, who have been called according to his purpose.*

This week spend some time researching the reasons for these basic translation differences and record which ones you agree with and why. This exercise challenges you to think through the logic of a text and in turn challenge the "heavyweights" (scholars/translators). I'll walk you through the steps to look at the Greek text online and you can consult commentaries for additional information.

If you have access to the Internet the following steps will help you find the Greek text at the Blue Letter Bible website and be able to compare it with the NASB and KJV.

1. Go to www.blueletterbible.org
2. Under the heading "Bible / Dictionary Search" enter "Romans 8:28" in the box.
3. Under "Version" select "NASB" from the pull down menu. This text makes "God" the subject of the verb *synergeo* ("work together").
4. Press the "Search" button.
5. You will see a cluster of six small boxes to the left of Romans 8:28. Click on the "C" box to bring up Romans 8:28 in both the New American Standard and the Greek text and a chart showing the New American Standard translation in the left-hand column and the corresponding Greek root words in the right-hand column.
6. Repeat the above process and instead of selecting the "NASB" as your version (step 3), select "KJV" (which makes "all things" the subject of the verb *synergeo* ("work together"). You'll be able to see the differences best if you open up two browser windows and view the information side by side.

Even if you're not a Greek scholar, a simple look at the text reveals that "God" (θεον: *theon*) only appears once in the Greek text and it is clearly in the accusative tense (the ν [Greek letter *nu*] at the end of the word shows this), the tense of a direct object. The challenge for translators is that Greek verbs don't have "gender," so determining the subject or implied subject here is fuzzy. Since most readers don't have the Greek skills to parse this sentence on their own, commentators and Greek experts can be a great help. One thing we can do is compare these translations with what we know to be true from other portions of Scripture. Does a suggested translation concur with the teaching of Scripture elsewhere?

Consult your commentaries on this verse and weigh the arguments with what you know about the clear teaching of Scripture elsewhere. Record your observations.

What did you notice as you compared the various translations? Are they as similar as you thought they would be? How and where do they vary from one another? Can you see how they arrived at their translation based on your research?

The bottom line on Romans 8:28 is that God is sovereign whether He directly causes something or whether He works through "all things," but "all things" of themselves do not order themselves for good apart from His agency. Even more fundamental is the fact that "things" do not order themselves. Order is an indication of an outside force acting upon things and leading to evidence of design in creation, and thus a creative and an active God!

OBSERVE the TEXT of SCRIPTURE

We've looked at John 3 once already, but this time watch in particular the scope of God's love.

READ John 3 and **CIRCLE** the word *world*.

John 3:16-17

16 *"For God so loved the world, that He gave His only begotten Son, that whoever believes in Him shall not perish, but have eternal life.*

17 *"For God did not send the Son into the world to judge the world, but that the world might be saved through Him.*

DISCUSS with your GROUP or PONDER on your own . . .

According to the text, who will have eternal life?

What is God's disposition toward the world according to John 3:16?

Why did God send His Son into the world?

We've already considered the condition of man under sin. What else can we add to our worldview based on God's example in sending His Son? How should this impact how we live?

ONE STEP FURTHER:

Check Out the Rest of the Story

In John 3 Jesus alludes to the story of Moses and the children of Israel in the wilderness as he talks about Himself and His mission on earth. To get the rest of this story, check out Numbers (yes, Numbers!) 21. Record your observations below.

Mindset
Learning and Living the Will of God
An Inductive Study of Romans 8

More things to think about . . .

In considering salvation we are faced with the character of a holy and compassionate God who gave His own Son to save a fallen world. We'll close out this week of study looking at the character of God in 2 Peter.

ONE STEP FURTHER:

Word Study: *apoleias/ apoleto*

There's a word group in 2 Peter 3:3-9. See if you can find where *apoleias* and *apoleto* occur and what they mean. Record your findings below.

OBSERVE the TEXT of SCRIPTURE

READ 2 Peter 3:3-9 and **UNDERLINE** all time words or phrases that refer to time.

2 Peter 3:3-9

3   Know this first of all, that in the last days mockers will come with their mocking, following after their own lusts,

4   and saying, "Where is the promise of His coming? For ever since the fathers fell asleep, all continues just as it was from the beginning of creation."

5   For when they maintain this, it escapes their notice that by the word of God the heavens existed long ago and the earth was formed out of water and by water,

6   through which the world at that time was destroyed, being flooded with water.

7   But by His word the present heavens and earth are being reserved for fire, kept for the day of judgment and destruction of ungodly men.

8   But do not let this one fact escape your notice, beloved, that with the Lord one day is like a thousand years, and a thousand years like one day.

9   The Lord is not slow about His promise, as some count slowness, but is patient toward you, not wishing for any to perish but for all to come to repentance.

DISCUSS with your GROUP or PONDER on your own . . .

How did destruction come upon the world during the time of Noah?

What is yet to come according to Peter?

What does Peter tell us about God's desire for all people?

Does your heart match God's heart on this? If so, how do you exhibit this in your behavior and lifestyle? If not, spend some time asking God to align your heart more and more with His. If you'd like, you can write a prayer below.

ONE STEP FURTHER:

Read Noah's Story in Genesis 6–9

Most people are familiar with Noah and the ark but for the full story of the condition of the world leading to God's judgment on His creation, read through Genesis 6–9. Record your observations below, noting why judgment came, what things changed after the flood, and what promises God made.

Digging Deeper

Working hard, enduring, and other sports metaphors . . .

So about this time you may be thinking, "Come on, God doesn't want us to just sit back and do nothing! What about all those great sports metaphors about fighting the good fight, boxing like there's no tomorrow, and running with endurance?"

   If you have some time this week, see what God's Word has to say about following hard after God. As you do, note who is being spoken to and what the context is. Is the author talking to people who are already in God's family? How does that change things? Record the verses for the passages you're looking at along with your observations. Also, if the passage starts with a "Therefore" go back to find out what it is there for!

Here are a few references to get you started.

1 Corinthians 9:24-27

Philippians 3:12-15

Hebrews 12:1-3

@THE END OF THE DAY . . .

You belong to God if the Spirit dwells in you. We have been adopted. We haven't "made the team," we've been brought into the family. As we close out our time of study this week, consider the peace that comes with acceptance into God's family and let this verse from John 10 minister to your soul:

My sheep hear My voice. and I know them, and they follow Me;
and I give eternal life to them, and they will never perish;
and no one will snatch them out of My hand.

My Father, who has given them to Me, is greater than all;
and no one is able to snatch them out of the Father's hand.

I and the Father are one.

—John 10:27-30

Living by the Spirit Today

But if anyone does not have the Spirit of Christ, he does not belong to Him.
—Romans 8:9b

So how does it all play out today? What does it mean for you and me to live by the Spirit? Does it mean I'm on the highway to Gehenna if I occasionally yell at other drivers or (heaven forbid!) get a speeding ticket? I sure hope not. We're going to consider closely this week what Paul is talking about in Romans 8. Up to this point, we've looked at a bunch of scriptures that should affect our world view—how we see the world we live in. Now we'll be even more intentional in seeing how right thinking and right action go together. We're also going to look at the assurance that comes from a life marked by walking in the Spirit. So, start thinking about where you're going! I'm going to take you to some scenic scriptural locations, but I love it when you can figure out where we might be heading on our tour!

AN OVERVIEW OF THE TEXT

Our base text for today is Romans 8:3-13. If you are pressed for time this week, soak in this passage and meditate on it.

OBSERVE the TEXT of SCRIPTURE

READ Romans 8:3-13. **UNDERLINE** every reference to *flesh* and **CIRCLE** every reference to *Spirit*.

Romans 8:3-13

3   *For what the Law could not do, weak as it was through the flesh, God did: sending His own Son in the likeness of sinful flesh and as an offering for sin, He condemned sin in the flesh,*

4   *so that the requirement of the Law might be fulfilled in us, who do not walk according to the flesh but according to the Spirit.*

5   *For those who are according to the flesh set their minds on the things of the flesh, but those who are according to the Spirit, the things of the Spirit.*

6   *For the mind set on the flesh is death, but the mind set on the Spirit is life and peace,*

7   *because the mind set on the flesh is hostile toward God; for it does not subject itself to the law of God, for it is not even able to do so,*

8   *and those who are in the flesh cannot please God.*

9   *However, you are not in the flesh but in the Spirit, if indeed the Spirit of God dwells in you. But if anyone does not have the Spirit of Christ, he does not belong to Him.*

10   *If Christ is in you, though the body is dead because of sin, yet the spirit is alive because of righteousness.*

11   *But if the Spirit of Him who raised Jesus from the dead dwells in you, He who raised Christ Jesus from the dead will also give life to your mortal bodies through His Spirit who dwells in you.*

12   *So then, brethren, we are under obligation, not to the flesh, to live according to the flesh—*

13   *for if you are living according to the flesh, you must die; but if by the Spirit you are putting to death the deeds of the body, you will live.*

DISCUSS with your GROUP or PONDER on your own . . .

What are your initial observations on the text?

ONE STEP FURTHER:

Word Study: Under Obligation

If you have some extra time this week, check into the phrase *under obligation* and see what the Greek behind it is and what else you can discover. Consider what our former obligation was and how having a new and better obligation necessarily affects it. *Can two mutually exclusive obligations have a hold on you?* Reason through the text and record what you find below.

What did you learn about those who are *according to the flesh*? What are they like? What do they do? What is their future?

What is their posture toward God?

Is there any benefit in life *according to the flesh*? Explain your answer.

What does the text tell us about life *according to the Spirit*?

What big evidence of belonging to God does Paul give here?

**Tight on Time?
Part 1—The Flesh**

If you're crazy tight on time this week, consider this: photocopy the text below, cut it out and carry it with you. Read it when you can: stop lights, when you get up, while you're unloading the dishwasher. Have it handy so you can read (and even perhaps memorize!) the text. This first part focuses mostly on "the flesh." Part 2 on the next page is the remainder of the passage which focuses more on "the Spirit."

5 *For those who are according to the flesh set their minds on the things of the flesh, but those who are according to the Spirit, the things of the Spirit.*

6 *For the mind set on the flesh is death, but the mind set on the Spirit is life and peace,*

7 *because the mind set on the flesh is hostile toward God; for it does not subject itself to the law of God, for it is not even able to do so,*

8 *and those who are in the flesh cannot please God.*

Mindset
Learning and Living the Will of God
An Inductive Study of Romans 8

Let's take a step back for a second as we reason through this: Who is Paul's audience?

Tight on Time?
Part 2—The Spirit

Here's the rest! If you're trying to memorize, marking the text's key words can be very helpful. Any time you see repetition or patterns, they are toeholds for climbing Memory Hill.

9 However, you are not in the flesh but in the Spirit, if indeed the Spirit of God dwells in you. But if anyone does not have the Spirit of Christ, he does not belong to Him.

10 If Christ is in you, though the body is dead because of sin, yet the spirit is alive because of righteousness.

11 But if the Spirit of Him who raised Jesus from the dead dwells in you, He who raised Christ Jesus from the dead will also give life to your mortal bodies through His Spirit who dwells in you.

12 So then, brethren, we are under obligation, not to the flesh, to live according to the flesh—

13 for if you are living according to the flesh, you must die; but if by the Spirit you are putting to death the deeds of the body, you will live.

Is everyone in the visible church "in Christ"? Explain your thinking.

How will this message be received differently for one who is "in Christ" versus one who is in the visible church but also "in the flesh"?

What is the big "If" in this section?

Before we jump into application, let's consider some other texts and see what else we can find to bring some more light to Romans 8.

Digging Deeper

1 John: So that you may know that you have eternal life . . .

If you have time this week, read through 1 John. John tells us he wrote this letter so that his readers can know that they have eternal life. He outlines basic characteristics present in people who are children of God. As you read, watch for these qualities and examine your own life.

What characterizes those who belong to God? (List the verses.)

How does your life line up with these truths in 1 John? Based on this, do you know that you have eternal life?

You can know Him today!

If you read through 1 John and came to the conclusion that you have a religion without a relationship, you don't have to stay there. You don't have to remain separated, you can enter a relationship with Jesus today.

The Bible tells us that we are all sinners—"for all have sinned and fall short of the glory of God" (Romans 3:23)—and death is coming to us because of this: "For the wages of sin is death, but the free gift of God is eternal life through Jesus Christ our Lord" (Romans 6:23).

As we've seen in our study, God didn't leave us in that situation, but sent Jesus to die in our place: "But God demonstrates His own love toward us, in that while we were yet sinners, Christ died for us" (Romans 5:8).

We accept that gift and enter into relationship with Him by faith: "For by grace you have been saved through faith; and that not of yourselves, *it is* the gift of God; not as a result of works, so that no one may boast. For we are His workmanship, created in Christ Jesus for good works, which God prepared beforehand so that we would walk in them" (Ephesians 2:8-10).

Two Trees . . .

Since we all find ourselves living in the world, it can be easy to think of walking by the flesh and walking by the Spirit as two ways of life that fundamentally coexist, perhaps like a hybrid car which runs sometimes on gas and other times on battery. But while we know from experience that none of us walks perfectly by the Spirit, Scripture teaches that we are fundamentally either *of and in* the Spirit or *of and in* the flesh.

Let's look at a few texts from Jesus and Paul that will help us understand the two natures a little better. Jesus talks about two kinds of trees—one good, one bad. We'll also look at more from Paul. But Jesus goes first!

OBSERVE the TEXT of SCRIPTURE

Jesus' teaching in this passage contains material that is also included in the Sermon on the Mount found in Matthew 5–7.

READ Luke 6:39-45. **CIRCLE** every reference to *good*. **BOX** every reference to *bad* or *evil*.

Luke 6:39-45

39 And He also spoke a parable to them: "A blind man cannot guide a blind man, can he? Will they not both fall into a pit?

40 "A pupil is not above his teacher; but everyone, after he has been fully trained, will be like his teacher.

41 "Why do you look at the speck that is in your brother's eye, but do not notice the log that is in your own eye?

42 "Or how can you say to your brother, 'Brother, let me take out the speck that is in your eye,' when you yourself do not see the log that is in your own eye? You hypocrite, first take the log out of your own eye, and then you will see clearly to take out the speck that is in your brother's eye.

43 "For there is no good tree which produces bad fruit, nor, on the other hand, a bad tree which produces good fruit.

44 "For each tree is known by its own fruit. For men do not gather figs from thorns, nor do they pick grapes from a briar bush.

45 "The good man out of the good treasure of his heart brings forth what is good; and the evil man out of the evil treasure brings forth what is evil; for his mouth speaks from that which fills his heart.

DISCUSS with your GROUP or PONDER on your own . . .

What are your initial observations on the text?

When is a pupil like his teacher? How does this help explain gaps between actual and godly behavior?

How is a tree known?

How are people like trees?

What does the mouth reveal about the heart?

How can we explain people (ourselves included!) who claim to know Christ but consistently produce bad fruit? Defend your answer.

FYI:

When will we be like Him?

We won't fully be like Him until we see Him as He is . . .

2   Beloved, now we are children of God, and it has not appeared as yet what we will be. We know that when He appears, we will be like Him, because we will see Him just as He is.

3   And everyone who has this hope fixed on Him purifies himself, just as He is pure.

—1 John 3:2-3

Mindset
Learning and Living the Will of God

An Inductive Study of Romans 8

More About Fruit . . .

Jesus talked about good trees bearing good fruit and bad trees bearing bad fruit. Paul gets a little more specific in Galatians where he attributes specific behavior to the Spirit and other specific behavior to the flesh. Let's take a look.

OBSERVE the TEXT of SCRIPTURE

READ Galatians 5:16, 19-23 and **UNDERLINE** what the flesh produces; **CIRCLE** the fruit of the Spirit.

Galatians 5:16, 19-23

16 But I say, walk by the Spirit, and you will not carry out the desire of the flesh.

19 Now the deeds of the flesh are evident, which are: immorality, impurity, sensuality,

20 idolatry, sorcery, enmities, strife, jealousy, outbursts of anger, disputes, dissensions, factions,

21 envying, drunkenness, carousing, and things like these, of which I forewarn you, just as I have forewarned you, that those who practice such things will not inherit the kingdom of God.

22 But the fruit of the Spirit is love, joy, peace, patience, kindness, goodness, faithfulness,

23 gentleness, self-control; against such things there is no law.

DISCUSS with your GROUP or PONDER on your own . . .

What are your initial observations on the text?

What deeds come from the flesh?

How do these compare with the fruit of the Spirit?

Can these coexist continually in a person's life? Explain.

Consider your own life for a moment: do some deeds of the flesh trip you up more than others?

How can we keep from carrying out the desires and deeds of the flesh?

Sure, God commands us to walk by the Spirit, but that again begs the questions *What exactly does this mean?* and *How exactly do I do it?* That's next on our agenda . . .

Think Oranges!

In verse 22, note that *fruit* is singular not plural. The picture is not of a tree with various kinds of fruit on it, but a tree that produces a fruit made up of these various qualities. Don't think apple, pear, banana, mango . . . think of a segmented orange, then examine their underlying unity by considering any pair of them: for example, is peace a form of self-control, kindness a type of good-ness, gentleness a kind of love? etc. The related segments are one fruit!

OBSERVE the TEXT of SCRIPTURE

READ Galatians 2:19-21 and **CIRCLE** every occurrence of *life* and *live(s)*. **UNDERLINE** references to *death* (died, crucified).

Galatians 2:19-21

19 *"For through the Law I died to the Law, so that I might live to God.*

20 *"I have been crucified with Christ; and it is no longer I who live, but Christ lives in me; and the life which I now live in the flesh I live by faith in the Son of God, who loved me and gave Himself up for me.*

21 *"I do not nullify the grace of God, for if righteousness comes through the Law, then Christ died needlessly."*

DISCUSS with your GROUP or PONDER on your own . . .

What are your initial observations on the text?

According to Paul, what happened to him?

How did this affect his mortal life, the life he *lives in the flesh*?

How does the phrase *in the flesh* differ here from how Paul uses it in Romans 8? How do you know?

So where does Paul's ability to *live to God* come from?

Is this available to us? Explain.

For all of our fussing over portions of the Bible we perceive as unclear, the line between the old and new life in Romans 8 is crystal clear. Paul's declaration ". . . if anyone does not have the Spirit of Christ, he does not belong to Him" (Romans 8:9b) is clear, disturbingly clear actually. But we need to remember that we are in a process. Recall Jesus' words in Luke 6:40: "A pupil is not above his teacher; but everyone, after he has been fully trained, will be like his teacher." That's a tall order, but when will this happen in the lives of true believers and what does this mean for us in the meantime? Let's look to 1 John.

OBSERVE the TEXT of SCRIPTURE

READ 1 John 3:1-3. **CIRCLE** every term of endearment (*beloved, children*) and **UNDERLINE** words related to *purity*.

1 John 3:1-3

1 *See how great a love the Father has bestowed on us, that we would be called children of God; and such we are. For this reason the world does not know us, because it did not know Him.*

2 *Beloved, now we are children of God, and it has not appeared as yet what we will be. We know that when He appears, we will be like Him, because we will see Him just as He is.*

3 *And everyone who has this hope fixed on Him purifies himself, just as He is pure.*

Mindset
Learning and Living the Will of God

An Inductive Study of Romans 8

DISCUSS with your GROUP or PONDER on your own . . .

What is the context of these verses? If you are familiar with 1 John, what do you know about it? Why does John say he's writing? (You'll find this in 1 John 5:13.)

Given the terms of endearment you marked, what does John seem to assume about his readers? What else supports this?

What does the hope of seeing Jesus do for us now?

Does this imply anything about our current state? If so, what?

How can these words comfort you in your current life situation?

Even those in Christ who bear the family resemblance will not be perfect until they see Him. Still, we need to consider the pattern of our lives to discern if we truly know Him. We need to be wise as serpents and innocent as doves (these are Jesus' words!) as we live life on the planet. Remember what the Bible teaches about us? We are fallen. And not all are who they claim to be. Let's check out what Jesus has to say in Matthew 7.

OBSERVE the TEXT of SCRIPTURE

READ Matthew 7:13-27. **CIRCLE** every word or phrase referring to true believers and **UNDERLINE** every word or phrase referring to those who show themselves to be false.

Matthew 7:13-27

13 "Enter through the narrow gate; for the gate is wide and the way is broad that leads to destruction, and there are many who enter through it.

14 "For the gate is small and the way is narrow that leads to life, and there are few who find it.

15 "Beware of the false prophets, who come to you in sheep's clothing, but inwardly are ravenous wolves.

16 "You will know them by their fruits. Grapes are not gathered from thorn bushes nor figs from thistles, are they?

17 "So every good tree bears good fruit, but the bad tree bears bad fruit.

18 "A good tree cannot produce bad fruit, nor can a bad tree produce good fruit.

19 "Every tree that does not bear good fruit is cut down and thrown into the fire.

20 "So then, you will know them by their fruits.

21 "Not everyone who says to Me, 'Lord, Lord,' will enter the kingdom of heaven, but he who does the will of My Father who is in heaven will enter.

22 "Many will say to Me on that day, 'Lord, Lord, did we not prophesy in Your name, and in Your name cast out demons, and in Your name perform many miracles?'

23 "And then I will declare to them, 'I never knew you; DEPART FROM ME, YOU WHO PRACTICE LAWLESSNESS.'

24 "Therefore everyone who hears these words of Mine and acts on them, may be compared to a wise man who built his house on the rock.

25 "And the rain fell, and the floods came, and the winds blew and slammed against that house; and yet it did not fall, for it had been founded on the rock.

26 "Everyone who hears these words of Mine and does not act on them, will be like a foolish man who built his house on the sand.

27 "The rain fell, and the floods came, and the winds blew and slammed against that house; and it fell—and great was its fall."

The Sermon on the Mount

In Matthew 5–7 we have a record of Jesus' extended teaching often referred to as The Sermon on the Mount. Among other teachings, it includes the Beatitudes (the "Blessed" statements) and the Lord's Prayer. My Pastor Joe refers to it as "Jesus' words for Jesus' people."

DISCUSS with your GROUP or PONDER on your own . . .

What are your initial observations on the text?

Learning and Living the Will of God

An Inductive Study of Romans 8

What pictures does Jesus use to describe different people and different ways?

Can you be a mango tree if you produce blueberries?

Let's think through this carefully. What does this section tell us about people (ourselves included!) who say they are one tree but produce another tree's fruit?

Does this mean we can work our way to God or is Jesus talking about something else? Explain your answer from Scripture.

Take some time to ask God what kind of fruit you are bearing. Be quiet with Him. Take a walk and record your thoughts below.

Because we're "works in progress" on earth, we need to consider how to submit to God's purifying work in our lives. Let's spend some time in Colossians to help us understand what Paul means when he speaks of walking by the Spirit.

OBSERVE the TEXT of SCRIPTURE

READ Colossians 1:9-12, 28-29 and **UNDERLINE** what Paul prays for the Colossians.

Colossians 1:9-12, 28-29

9 *For this reason also, since the day we heard of it, we have not ceased to pray for you and to ask that you may be filled with the knowledge of His will in all spiritual wisdom and understanding,*

10 *so that you will walk in a manner worthy of the Lord, to please Him in all respects, bearing fruit in every good work and increasing in the knowledge of God;*

11 *strengthened with all power, according to His glorious might, for the attaining of all steadfastness and patience; joyously*

12 *giving thanks to the Father, who has qualified us to share in the inheritance of the saints in Light.*

28 *We proclaim Him, admonishing every man and teaching every man with all wisdom, so that we may present every man complete in Christ.*

29 *For this purpose also I labor, striving according to His power, which mightily works within me.*

DISCUSS with your GROUP or PONDER on your own . . .

What are your initial observations on the text?

FYI:

Learning to Pray

When Jesus' disciples asked Him to teach them to pray, He did just that. We can learn from His example, but we can also learn by observing other prayers in Scripture. I'll never forget the card I received from my Bible study teacher and mentor who told me she was praying Colossians 1:9-12 for me. I have often re-read that card over the years and been reminded of her prayers and God's faithfulness in answering. Is there someone in your life you can be praying Colossians 1:9-12 for today?

ONE STEP FURTHER:

Word Study

Okay, there are so many options for word studies in this dense section that I hate to pick just one. Identify one or more that you'd like to interact with and go to it. Record your findings below and don't forget to consider the implications, if any, of how this informs our desire to walk in the Spirit.

Learning and Living the Will of God

An Inductive Study of Romans 8

What does Paul specifically pray for these people?

Where does the power come from? How can we submit to God in this process? How can we actively participate?

How can we increase in our knowledge of God?

What else can we do?

What is Paul's goal for those he's teaching and investing in?

Is there anything Paul prays for the Colossians that you need to begin praying for yourself and others?

ONE STEP FURTHER:

Word Study: Complete

In Colossians 1:28 Paul says he wants to present every man *complete in Christ.* If you have some extra time this week, see what you can find out about the Greek word for *complete.* Where else is it used? How else is it translated? What is Paul getting at? Record your findings below.

After telling the Colossians what he is praying for them, Paul sets out to give them both a "What Is" and a "How To" section in Colossians 3:1-17.

OBSERVE the TEXT of SCRIPTURE

READ Colossians 3:1-17 and **UNDERLINE** everything Paul tells them to do.

Colossians 3:1-17

1   Therefore if you have been raised up with Christ, keep seeking the things above, where Christ is, seated at the right hand of God.

2   Set your mind on the things above, not on the things that are on earth.

3   For you have died and your life is hidden with Christ in God.

4   When Christ, who is our life, is revealed, then you also will be revealed with Him in glory.

5   Therefore consider the members of your earthly body as dead to immorality, impurity, passion, evil desire, and greed, which amounts to idolatry.

6   For it is because of these things that the wrath of God will come upon the sons of disobedience,

7   and in them you also once walked, when you were living in them.

8   But now you also, put them all aside: anger, wrath, malice, slander, and abusive speech from your mouth.

9   Do not lie to one another, since you laid aside the old self with its evil practices,

10 and have put on the new self who is being renewed to a true knowledge according to the image of the One who created him—

11 a renewal in which there is no distinction between *Greek and Jew*, *circumcised and uncircumcised*, *barbarian, Scythian, slave and freeman*, but *Christ is all, and in all.*

12 So, as those who have been chosen of God, holy and beloved, put on a heart of compassion, kindness, humility, gentleness and patience;

13 bearing with one another, and forgiving each other, whoever has a complaint against anyone; just as the Lord forgave you, so also should you.

14 Beyond all these things put on love, which is the perfect bond of unity.

15 Let the peace of Christ rule in your hearts, to which indeed you were called in one body; and be thankful.

16 Let the word of Christ richly dwell within you, with all wisdom teaching and admonishing one another with *psalms* and *hymns* and *spiritual songs*, singing with thankfulness in your hearts to God.

17 Whatever you do in word or deed, do all in the name of the Lord Jesus, giving thanks through Him to God the Father.

FYI:

The Imperative Mood

The Greek imperative mood communicates a command. It's neither a proposition, request, nor suggestion; it doesn't call its hearers to think but to choose and do (obey). If you take some time to check out the Greek verbs, you'll notice this section of Colossians is full of imperatives.

Mindset

Learning and Living the Will of God

An Inductive Study of Romans 8

DISCUSS with your GROUP or PONDER on your own . . .

What are your initial observations on the text?

What important word opens this section? What is it referring to?

What is Paul's readers' situation?

Look carefully at the verbs in this section. What actions does Paul say they should take? (This is a good set of imperatives to list.)

What does Paul say about our relationship to others?

What does the Word of God have to do with this? How does our relationship to the Word of God help us both walk in the Spirit ourselves and encourage others to do the same?

Is there anything in this section you need to focus on either putting on or taking off? Explain.

ONE STEP FURTHER:

Earthly Wisdom and Heavenly Wisdom

Take some time this week to read James 3:13-18 and consider what is ruling your heart. I find this is especially helpful when I'm in a decision-making process. Is there peace in my heart or bitter jealousy and strife? It can be very, very telling. As you read, list what marks godly wisdom and what marks worldly wisdom. The next time you're faced with a decision, consider which you are living by.

Mindset

Learning and Living the Will of God

An Inductive Study of Romans 8

Digging Deeper

Guarding our Hearts from the Wolves

This week we've focused our attention on the life that pleases God, the life lived by the Spirit. But the Word also talks in depth about how to discern wolves. If you have time this week, examine the following Scriptures for information about those who walk according to the flesh and how to identify them. Please, examine other appropriate Scripture passages as well. Consider what characterizes these people and what ramifications that has on us. How do we respond? How do we guard our hearts? How do we tell the difference between baby sheep and mature wolves dressed up as sheep? This is important because wolves like to hang around and prey on sheep.

Matthew 23:1-12

2 Timothy 3:1-5

FYI:

Philippians 4:4-9

4 Rejoice in the Lord always; again I will say, rejoice!

5 Let your gentle spirit be known to all men. The Lord is near.

6 Be anxious for nothing, but in everything by prayer and supplication with thanksgiving let your requests be made known to God.

7 And the peace of God, which surpasses all comprehension, will guard your hearts and your minds in Christ Jesus.

8 Finally, brethren, whatever is true, whatever is honorable, whatever is right, whatever is pure, whatever is lovely, whatever is of good repute, if there is any excellence and if anything worthy of praise, dwell on these things.

9 The things you have learned and received and heard and seen in me, practice these things, and the God of peace will be with you.

@THE END OF THE DAY . . .

We're closing in on the end of our time together in Romans 8. Has your thinking changed in regard to the nature of man? The character of God? What it means to live life in the Spirit? Spend some quiet time with God and consider if your thinking today is different from what it was before you began your study of Romans 8. Record below what God brings to mind.

Lesson Six

Present Help, Future Hope

*But if the Spirit of Him who raised Jesus from the dead dwells in you,
He who raised Christ Jesus from the dead will also give life to your
mortal bodies through His Spirit who dwells in you.*
—Romans 8:11

My favorite television show of all time ended recently. The main character walked into the church for his father's funeral and to his utter shock found not his father but his own body lying in the coffin. The church featured a wide variety of stained glass religious symbols. All the important people in the protagonist's life—all dead themselves from different times—met him at the church and together they walked into the light. What was on the other side? They didn't know, but they were all ready to "move on." Ah, there seemed to be hope, there was light . . . but on the other side of the door there was only more make believe.

The Christian hope, the biblical perspective, offers the Holy Spirit's present help and true hope, not a vague "light" concocted by creative writers but a resurrection of the body and life forever made possible by the powerful work of a sovereign God. Let's walk toward the light this week . . . the real light!

"I am the Light of the world; he who follows Me will not walk in the darkness, but will have the Light of life."
—Jesus

ONE STEP FURTHER:

Using the Plumbline

I love Precept Ministries' plumbline logo. A plumbline is a tool carpenters use to see if they're building straight (plumb). It shows true vertical—everything in a building project is measured against that truth. The Bible is our plumbline—everything in our lives should be measured against the truth of God's Word. My friend, when we engage our culture it is critical that we know truth so we can identify false when we see it and not be swept away by clever lies.

It can be tempting to grab our plumblines and run for cover into the safety of a believing community and just try to keep ourselves unsoiled from the world. Hide the kids, close the windows, cut the Internet and wait for Jesus. But Jesus calls us to engage. We are to go and make disciples. We are to be a city set on a hill, a lamp on a stand, salt of the earth. We need to know the truth and have our minds renewed so we can think clearly as we live as strangers in a fallen world.

If you have some extra time this week, think through some of the common beliefs of our culture that sound good but don't line up with Scripture. Record your thoughts below.

Mindset
Learning and Living the Will of God

An Inductive Study of Romans 8

Lesson Six: **Present Help, Future Hope**

In Romans 8 we have seen so much doctrine. We've seen what man is and what God is. We've seen how man got himself into the mess of sin and how God gets him out. We've seen what our sin has done to the planet, but we've also seen how God changes us through the work of His Spirit and how all of this should affect the way we think, live, and carry on day after day. In theological terms, so far we've touched on the doctrines of man, God, sin, salvation, and sanctification.

FYI:

Knowledge and Love

Knowledge puffs up, but love builds up.
    −1 Corinthians 8:1b NIV

REVIEW

When we learn truth and the Spirit applies it we change. As we start off today, take some time to consider how God's Word has impacted your world view in the following areas. Consider how your thinking and behavior have been altered. Remember Paul's words to the Corinthian church, "Knowledge puffs up, but love builds up." Whenever we add knowledge, we need to apply what we know in our lives.

What I've learned about man . . .

What I've learned about God . . .

What I've learned about creation . . .

What I've learned about sin . . .

What I've learned about salvation . . .

What I've learned about sanctification . . .

Questions I still have . . .

It's Okay to Still Have Questions

One of the most important lessons I learned in college was that it is okay to have questions. God is big enough and smart enough for my questions. For many questions, you'll discover answers as you study the Scriptures and pursue God, but there are some questions we won't have answered in this lifetime . . . and that's okay. We have a rational faith and an omniscient God. I bring Him all my questions knowing that He has the answers. And I can trust that He's good in things He has not revealed and in things I can't understand or comprehend.

Deuteronomy 29:29 tells us "The secret things belong to the LORD our God, but the things revealed belong to us and to our sons forever, that we may observe all the words of this law." Some things He hasn't revealed. To me this is comforting and it leaves me joyfully and hopefully expecting His best.

I don't need to know everything God knows in order to be able to rest in Him. If I know He is sovereign and I know He is good, I can rest. I don't have to worry that my questions will be His undoing—that somehow I'll come up with the one question that destroys the house of cards! Some questions aren't answered here because He has no intention of answering them here. He is Lord and He owes us nothing which makes the amount He *does* reveal to us utterly amazing and the amount He *doesn't* our hope.

Mindset
Learning and Living the Will of God

An Inductive Study of Romans 8

OBSERVE the TEXT of SCRIPTURE

READ all of Romans 8 to put yourself in context. We're going to concentrate first on verses 26-27. Later in our lesson we'll zero in on verses 31-39. Right now as we observe, **CIRCLE** every word relating to the *Spirit* and **UNDERLINE** every word that talks about us *(our, we, saints).*

Romans 8:26-27

26 *In the same way the Spirit also helps our weakness; for we do not know how to pray as we should, but the Spirit Himself intercedes for us with groanings too deep for words;*

27 *and He who searches the hearts knows what the mind of the Spirit is, because He intercedes for the saints according to the will of God.*

DISCUSS with your GROUP or PONDER on your own . . .

What are your initial observations on the text?

What questions do you think we need to ask?

What does the Spirit do? How does he make up for what is lacking in us?

What are we lacking? What is our weakness?

In verse 27, we have two pronouns with unclear antecedents. Who is the "He" of the first part of verse 27? Who is the "He" of the second? List the possibilities below, then we'll think through it together

In order to help us lock in on who's who, let's list everyone clearly mentioned in verses 26 and 27.

Is verse 26 clear about who intercedes for us? Who is that?

Does anyone else intercede for us according to Romans 8? Who and in what context?

What do you learn about Jesus' intercession in Romans 8:34 and Hebrews 7:25?

Based on the text, do you think the "He" of "He intercedes for the saints according to the will of God" is the Holy Spirit or Jesus? Why?

ONE STEP FURTHER:

Word Study: Intercedes

What are the different Greek words for *intercedes* in Romans 8 and elsewhere in the New Testament? Take some time this week to investigate and record your findings below.

Digging Deeper

What else do we know about the Holy Spirit?

He is the least mentioned member of the Trinity, but His presence in us marks us as belonging to God. If you have some time this week, run some concordance searches and scrub the Scriptures for additional things you can learn about the Holy Spirit.

    Here are a few questions to get you thinking: *Where do we see Him? What else is He called? What was His role in the Old Testament and how does it compare with His role in the New? What, if any, role does He play in the lives of unbelievers? How does He help believers?*

Have fun and record your findings (with references!) below.

What about "He who searches the hearts"? Let's reason through this.

Is this "He" the Holy Spirit? Why/why not?

Is this Jesus? Why/why not?

Is this God, the Father? Why/why not?

Where else in Scripture are there references to One who searches hearts? How does this inform what you've concluded so far?

What is the bottom line of Romans 8:26-27? What is our problem? How does God solve it for us?

There is so much application waiting in Romans 8:26-27, but before we go there, let's examine a couple of other passages on prayer that will shed more light on what we have learned so far.

OBSERVE the TEXT of SCRIPTURE

READ 1 John 5:13-15. **UNDERLINE** every occurrence of *know* and **CIRCLE** every *if*.

1 John 5:13-15

13 *These things I have written to you who believe in the name of the Son of God, so that you may know that you have eternal life.*

14 *This is the confidence which we have before Him, that, if we ask anything according to His will, He hears us.*

15 *And if we know that He hears us in whatever we ask, we know that we have the requests which we have asked from Him.*

DISCUSS with your GROUP or PONDER on your own . . .

What can we know?

What do we learn from the *ifs* in the text? How is God's will involved?

Digging Deeper

What else does the Word teach about prayer?

If you can, take some time this week to see what else the Bible teaches about prayer. Again, a great place to start is with a concordance to find where else prayer is mentioned in the Bible. Remember, Scripture always interprets Scripture so the more widely you read, the more sides of the jewel you will see. Record your findings and applications below. As you read, watch for synonyms to widen your search.

How hung up do you get on being "in the know" about God's will?

What is God's will?

Sometimes it's a little confusing for us, but so often it is as clear as the words on this page. Take some time to see what the Bible says about God's specific will and record your findings below. Here's an example to get you started:

• 1 Thessalonians 5:18 - ". . . in everything give thanks; for **this is God's will** for you in Christ Jesus."

If you *know* the Spirit intercedes even though you don't know the details of what He is praying on your behalf, how can this radically change your outlook and behavior?

Do you ever fear that you haven't prayed enough? Does this text comfort you at all? How?

Before we move on, let's consider one more text on prayer to round out our study from a manward perspective. We know the Spirit intercedes for us, but what does Jesus tell us about how and what we should pray? Let's look to Jesus' teaching in Matthew 6 for some answers.

OBSERVE the TEXT of SCRIPTURE

READ Matthew 6:5-15. **UNDERLINE** everything we are *not to do* and **CIRCLE** phrases that tell us what *to do*.

Matthew 6:5-15

5   *"When you pray, you are not to be like the hypocrites; for they love to stand and pray in the synagogues and on the street corners so that they may be seen by men. Truly I say to you, they have their reward in full.*

6   *"But you, when you pray, go into your inner room, close your door and pray to your Father who is in secret, and your Father who sees what is done in secret will reward you.*

7   *"And when you are praying, do not use meaningless repetition as the Gentiles do, for they suppose that they will be heard for their many words.*

8   *"So do not be like them; for your Father knows what you need before you ask Him.*

9 *"Pray, then, in this way:*

'Our Father who is in heaven,

Hallowed be Your name.

10 *'Your kingdom come.*

Your will be done,

On earth as it is in heaven.

11 *'Give us this day our daily bread.*

12 *'And forgive us our debts, as we also have forgiven our debtors.*

13 *'And do not lead us into temptation, but deliver us from evil. [For Yours is the kingdom and the power and the glory forever. Amen.]'*

14 *"For if you forgive others for their transgressions, your heavenly Father will also forgive you.*

15 *"But if you do not forgive others, then your Father will not forgive your transgressions."*

DISCUSS with your GROUP or PONDER on your own . . .

What is the key word in this text? How did you identify it?

Did you notice any other repeated words that are important? If so what and why are they important?

What are some characteristics of misguided prayer? What do people do and why? (Answer from the text.)

Mindset
Learning and Living the Will of God

An Inductive Study of Romans 8

Lesson Six: **Present Help, Future Hope**

What does Jesus say His people should do when they pray and why?

How does Jesus say we should pray? Do you notice any general categories? If so, what are they?

What does this text say about God's will?

How does this compare with how we typically talk about God's will? How can we correct our prayers to be more biblical? How can this affect our thinking?

How important is it that we forgive others? Why?

Is there any unforgiveness you need to confess and repent of today? If so, take some time to meditate on these verses and ask the Lord to forgive you and change your heart.

Take a walk and reflect on the gift of His forgiveness. Are you living fully in the light of the finished work of Christ? How does your life reflect His forgiveness? Record your thoughts below.

As we circle for our final approach it's time to focus on the last verses of Romans 8, some of the most encouraging and heartening words ever written. I'm half inclined not to ask any questions but to just beg you to memorize this. But alas, since Paul fills his final section with questions, how can we do anything less?

OBSERVE the TEXT of SCRIPTURE

READ Romans 8:31-39 and **MARK** every reference to *God*. Then **MARK** every reference to *Jesus Christ*. Don't forget to include pronouns. Finally, **CIRCLE** every reference to the people of God.

Romans 8:31-39

31 What then shall we say to these things? If God is for us, who is against us?

32 He who did not spare His own Son, but delivered Him over for us all, how will He not also with Him freely give us all things?

33 Who will bring a charge against God's elect? God is the one who justifies;

34 who is the one who condemns? Christ Jesus is He who died, yes, rather who was raised, who is at the right hand of God, who also intercedes for us.

35 Who will separate us from the love of Christ? Will tribulation, or distress, or persecution, or famine, or nakedness, or peril, or sword?

36 Just as it is written,

"FOR YOUR SAKE WE ARE BEING PUT TO DEATH ALL DAY LONG;

WE WERE CONSIDERED AS SHEEP TO BE SLAUGHTERED."

37 But in all these things we overwhelmingly conquer through Him who loved us.

38 For I am convinced that neither death, nor life, nor angels, nor principalities, nor things present, nor things to come, nor powers,

39 nor height, nor depth, nor any other created thing, will be able to separate us from the love of God, which is in Christ Jesus our Lord.

FYI

Big WIN!

The famous "Swoosh" logo on shoes and sports apparel everywhere alludes back to Nike, the Greek goddess of victory. The Swoosh is a graphic representation of her wing and the name is taken directly from the Greek word for victory, *nikē*. It's a great name for a company selling competitive edge.

Christians have a better word . . . *huper-nikaō*. Translated *overwhelmingly conquer* in Romans 8:37, "hyper-conquer" trumps the single Swoosh. Followers of Christ not only win they also win big. We hyper- (*huper*) conquer (*nikaō*) through Him who loved us. We slightly prefer "hyper-" to "more than" not just because it transliterates better but also because it's a superlative degree *of conquering* whereas "more than" implies *something better than [above] conquering* and we're not told what that is. The NAU's (1995 NASB) "overwhelmingly conquer" is a great translation. Next time I see the Swoosh, I'm setting my mind on this truth!

Lesson Six: **Present Help, Future Hope**

DISCUSS with your GROUP or PONDER on your own . . .

What does Paul tell us about God the Father in this passage? Who is He for? What has He done for us?

ONE STEP FURTHER:

Word Study: Separate

If you have time this week, find the Greek word for *separate* and see where else and how else it is used in the New Testament. Record your findings below.

What do we learn about Jesus? What did He do for us? What does He continue to do for us?

Have you identified any key words in this passage? What were they and why do you see them as key?

How specifically do we know that God is for us? What evidence does Paul give in the text?

In spite of all the threats posed by circumstances and events in life and death, what will never happen to God's elect?

Does this mean everything will always be smooth sailing? Explain your answer from this text and any others you know that are relevant.

Digging Deeper

No Separation Anxiety

Although life on the planet comes with tribulation, distress, persecution and the like, nothing can separate us from Christ if we are "in Him." He is over it all and because of this we can live at peace even when circumstances try to tell us we can't. If you have time this week, look more closely at what we are promised victory over because of our relationship with Jesus Christ. Don't get overburdened in this, but if you have time, look into a few of the things we no longer have to fear. Will we encounter some? Yes, but they will never be able to separate us from the love of God which is in Christ.

Tribulation

Distress

Persecution

Famine

Nakedness

Peril

Sword

Death

Angels

Principalities

Powers

Any created thing

Is there a particular situation in which you need to hold on to the truth that "we overwhelmingly conquer through Him who loved us"? If so, put that down here along with how you can live in the light of this truth.

How can these truths change the trajectory of a life?

So at this point we know that through Christ we overwhelmingly conquer, but we can't get around the fact that the text also refers to us being "put to death all day long." If you studied Hebrews 11 with us, you know that while most of the accounts end well in a temporal sense, the chapter closes with people being sawn in two, stoned to death, and dying by the sword. None of these sound like overwhelming victories. With this in mind, let's look at some more texts.

First we'll look at Paul's first letter to the church at Corinth where he talks about the necessity of Christ's resurrection to the Christian life. If Jesus is still in the grave, my friends, it is time to close the doors and invest our tithes and offerings elsewhere. Then as we close our study time we'll jump to the end of the Book, to the Revelation of Jesus Christ to John, as we glimpse at the final victory. If you've never read Revelation, this text may unsettle you.

OBSERVE the TEXT of SCRIPTURE

READ 1 Corinthians 15:16-26 and **MARK** every reference to *Christ*. **CIRCLE** every reference to *death*, including synonyms.

1 Corinthians 15:16-26

16 For if the dead are not raised, not even Christ has been raised;

17 and if Christ has not been raised, your faith is worthless; you are still in your sins.

18 Then those also who have fallen asleep in Christ have perished.

19 If we have hoped in Christ in this life only, we are of all men most to be pitied.

20 But now Christ has been raised from the dead, the first fruits of those who are asleep.

21 For since by a man came death, by a man also came the resurrection of the dead.

22 For as in Adam all die, so also in Christ all will be made alive.

23 But each in his own order: Christ the first fruits, after that those who are Christ's at His coming,

24 then comes the end, when He hands over the kingdom to the God and Father, when He has abolished all rule and all authority and power.

25 For He must reign until He has put all His enemies under His feet.

26 The last enemy that will be abolished is death.

DISCUSS with your GROUP or PONDER on your own . . .

What is Paul's line of reasoning here with reference to the resurrection of Jesus? Have you ever thought about the importance of the resurrection in these terms before?

Lesson Six: **Present Help, Future Hope**

If Christ has not been raised, what are the specific implications for us? Answer from the text and then apply it to examples from your life.

What did you learn from marking *death* and its synonyms?

What does Christ do to death? How does this fit with what we have learned so far in Romans 8?

How can this change your perspective?

In Revelation, John describes a vision of the future that the risen Christ has revealed to him. Read this text carefully.

OBSERVE the TEXT of SCRIPTURE

READ Revelation 21:1-8. **CIRCLE** every occurrence of *new*. **MARK** every reference to *God*.

Revelation 21:1-8

1   Then I saw a new heaven and a new earth; for the first heaven and the first earth passed away, and there is no longer any sea.

2   And I saw the holy city, new Jerusalem, coming down out of heaven from God, made ready as a bride adorned for her husband.

3   And I heard a loud voice from the throne, saying, "Behold, the tabernacle of God is among men, and He will dwell among them, and they shall be His people, and God Himself will be among them,

4   and He will wipe away every tear from their eyes; and there will no longer be any death; there will no longer be any mourning, or crying, or pain; the first things have passed away."

5   And He who sits on the throne said, "Behold, I am making all things new." And He said, "Write, for these words are faithful and true."

6   Then He said to me, "It is done. I am the Alpha and the Omega, the beginning and the end. I will give to the one who thirsts from the spring of the water of life without cost.

7   "He who overcomes will inherit these things, and I will be his God and he will be My son.

8   "But for the cowardly and unbelieving and abominable and murderers and immoral persons and sorcerers and idolaters and all liars, their part will be in the lake that burns with fire and brimstone, which is the second death."

DISCUSS with your GROUP or PONDER on your own . . .

Does this text challenge preconceived ideas you have about eternity with God? What lines up? Do you need to correct anything?

The Book with a Blessing

Revelation is the one book in the Bible that promises a blessing to those who read, hear, and heed its words. The Greek word behind *heed* is *tēreō* which means to keep or obey. Heed isn't a common word in our language today, but I think it's worth keeping around if for no other reason than to remind ourselves that when it comes to God's revelation, both with respect to Revelation and in the rest of His Book, we need to both read AND heed! Studying and reading should never be ends in themselves. They are but steps along the path of obedience.

Read it and heed it!

What will fundamentally change? What things "will no longer be"?

What has been undone? Think back to what was lost in the Garden of Eden and compare this picture with the picture we had in Genesis 3.

The future picture continues in Revelation 22 where a familiar tree reappears on the scene . . .

OBSERVE the TEXT of SCRIPTURE

READ Revelation 22:1-5. **MARK** every reference to *God*. **UNDERLINE** words referring to His people.

Revelation 22:1-5

1   Then he showed me a river of the water of life, clear as crystal, coming from the throne of God and of the Lamb,

2   in the middle of its street. On either side of the river was the tree of life, bearing twelve kinds of fruit, yielding its fruit every month; and the leaves of the tree were for the healing of the nations.

3   There will no longer be any curse; and the throne of God and of the Lamb will be in it, and His bond-servants will serve Him;

4   they will see His face, and His name will be on their foreheads.

5   And there will no longer be any night; and they will not have need of the light of a lamp nor the light of the sun, because the Lord God will illumine them; and they will reign forever and ever.

FYI:

The Twist at the End of the Story

I'll never forget the first time I read through the book of Revelation for myself. I was sobered by Jesus' words to the churches about enduring to the end, I loved the glimpse into heaven's courts, and I was plain lost for most of the middle chapters of the book. The fog of those chapters stood in such stark contrast to the clarity I saw in the final chapters of the book. What shook me, though, was while the text was clear it wasn't what I expected. Maybe you'll relate to this too.

I had always thought of heaven as a place "out there" where we live with Jesus forever. Looking back it's not that I had been taught incorrectly, I guess I just never had the whole story. Jesus told His disciples that He was going to prepare a place for them, I just never realized that "the place" eventually comes down to earth.

It makes sense, though, doesn't it? As Paul tells us, "the creation itself also will be set free from its slavery to corruption into the freedom of the glory of the children of God" (Romans 8:21).

DISCUSS with your GROUP or PONDER on your own . . .

What familiar tree reappears? When was it last referred to in the Bible? What was significant about this tree?

What else "will no longer be" according to verse 3? Considering Genesis 3 what does this undo?

Do you remember what God commanded man to do in Genesis 1:26-28? What frustrated this?

What does Revelation say God's bond-servants will do when God makes everything right again?

@THE END OF THE DAY . . .

As we bring this study to a close, take some time to quietly read Romans 8. Then take a walk and think about what you've read and what you have studied in these past weeks. Think through what we've learned from God's Word about God, creation, man, sin, salvation, sanctification, and our future hope in Jesus. Ask God to cement in your heart one or two specific truths from His Word that have affected you the most. Record them below.

For in hope we have been saved, but hope that is seen is not hope; for who hopes for what he already sees? But if we hope for what we do not see, with perseverance we wait eagerly for it.

–Romans 8:24-25

He who testifies to these things says, "Yes, I am coming quickly." Amen. Come, Lord Jesus.

–Revelation 22:20

Helpful Study Tools

The New How to Study Your Bible
Eugene, Oregon: Harvest House
Publishers

The New Inductive Study Bible
Eugene, Oregon: Harvest House
Publishers

Logos Bible Software
Available at www.logos.com.

Greek Word Study Tools

Kittel, G., Friedrich, G., & Bromiley,
G.W.
*Theological Dictionary of the New
Testament, Abridged* (also known as
Little Kittel)
Grand Rapids, Michigan: W.B.
Eerdmans Publishing Company

Zodhiates, Spiros
*The Complete Word Study Dictionary:
New Testament*
Chattanooga, Tennessee: AMG
Publishers

Hebrew Word Study Tools

Harris, R.L., Archer, G.L., & Walker,
B.K.
*Theological Wordbook of the Old
Testament* (also known as TWOT)
Chicago, Illinois: Moody Press

Zodhiates, Spiros
*The Complete Word Study Dictionary:
Old Testament*
Chattanooga, Tennessee: AMG
Publishers

General Word Study Tools

Strong, James
*The New Strong's Exhaustive
Concordance of the Bible*
Nashville, Tennessee: Thomas Nelson

Recommended Commentary Sets

Expositor's Bible Commentary
Grand Rapids, Michigan: Zondervan

NIV Application Commentary
Grand Rapids, Michigan: Zondervan

The New American Commentary
Nashville, Tennessee: Broadman and
Holman Publishers

Advanced Commentary on Romans

Moo, Douglas
*The New International Commentary on
the New Testament: The Epistle to the
Romans*
Grand Rapids, MI: W.B. Eerdmans
Publishing Company

HOW TO DO AN ONLINE WORD STUDY

For use with www.blueletterbible.org

1. Type in Bible verse. Change the version to NASB95. Click the "Search" button.

2. When you arrive at the next screen, you will see a button labeled "Tools" to the left of your verse.

   Hover over the "Tools" button and a list will pop up.

   Click the first button on the pop-up list—"Interlinear"—to take you to the concordance link.

3. Click on the Strong's number which is the link to the original word in Greek or Hebrew.

Clicking this number will bring up another screen that will give you a brief definition of the word as well as list every occurrence of the Greek word in the New Testament or Hebrew word in the Old Testament. Before running to a dictionary definition, scan places where it's used in Scripture and examine the general contexts.

We'd Love to Hear From You!

If you found this study helpful please take

a moment to share your thoughts.

Leave a Testimonial

https://www.pamgillaspieshop.com/products/mindset-romans-8

OR

Take a Short Survey

https://bit.ly/MindsetBookSurvey